# Messiah

المسيح

The Jesus of the Qur'an and the Gospels

James Appel, MD

*In memory of*
*Mahamat Saleh Abakar*

"And We did not send any
except men before you whom We inspired,
so ask the people who
have received the Reminder
if you do not know.
With proofs and the scriptures.
And We sent down to you
the Reminder to reveal to the people
what was sent to them,
and perhaps they will THINK."

Qur'an 16:43-44

# Contents

# Preface

Christians and Muslims differ about a lot of things. Most of them don't pose a real barrier to understanding. However, when it comes to Jesus the Messiah, the differences cut right to the heart for believers from both monotheistic faiths. Christians insist Jesus is the Son of God, a divine member of the Trinity and was crucified and died on a cross. Muslims insist he was just a prophet, a messenger like many others before and after him, he was certainly not the Son of God and definitely not one of three in a trinity of gods. Irreconcilable, right?

Maybe, but could it be that years of wars, centuries of tradition and layer upon layer of cultural differences have obscured the real Jesus for both Muslims and Christians? Is the Christian Jesus the Jesus of the Gospels? Is the Muslim Jesus (*Isa al Masih*) the real Jesus of the Qur'an? Could it be that both have been tainted with time? Could it be that when one looks back at the ancient Holy Books that the two Jesus' are actually not that different? Could it be that they're the same?

This book takes as its starting point an outrageous assumption: that both Christianity and Islam at their core are true. In other words, when one strips away years of tradition and culture and returns to the sources of both religions, the Qur'an and the Gospels, one finds that what appears to be irreconcilable differences concerning Jesus the Messiah are simply misunderstandings.

So, this book is not for everybody. If you believe that you and your religion are right and everybody else is wrong, this book is not for you. If you think that what your pastor, mullah, priest or imam says is the only interpretation of your scriptures, then this book is not for you. If you put greater emphasis on tradition and culture than truth and scripture, then this book is not for you.

However, if you believe that God is greater than any one person or group's understanding of who He is, than this book is for you. If you think the only source of truth are the Holy Books, then this book is for you. If you aren't afraid to have your preconceived notions questioned, then this book is for you. If you aren't afraid of going against the tide of mainstream tradition, then this book is for you. If you desire to know God more than please your religious leaders, then this book is for you.

In this book I have attempted the impossible: I've tried to look at the Qur'an and the Gospels without bias or preconceived notions. Obviously, this is impossible. No one is unbiased. With the Qur'an it was easier because I wasn't raised in a Muslim tradition so I was able to come to Islam's Holy Book with a fairly open mind. I was very surprised at what I found.

With the Gospels, it was more difficult to be objective since I was raised in a conservative Seventh-day Adventist home, the son of a Pastor. However, over the years I have learned the value of being critical and listening to other perspectives. A big help in my learning to see past tradition and culture in interpreting the Gospels has been being exposed to Islam by working in the Republic of Chad since 2004 and by reading the Qur'an multiple times.

Because of my studies on this subject I have come to believe that the same inspired truths about Jesus are in both the Qur'an and the Gospels. So how do I reconcile the apparent contradictions, especially concerning Jesus the Messiah? Simple, by stripping away my preconceived ideas of Jesus in the Gospels and reading them again with fresh eyes. And what I've found is that I have nothing to be ashamed of in being inspired by both the Qur'an and the Gospels. Why? Because Jesus is the same in both.

Don't believe me? Well, at least give me a chance to explain myself...

**NOTE:** Key Arabic phrases are included in italics enclosed in parenthesis. Example: Jesus the Messiah (*Isa al-Masih*).

# Introduction:
# It's About Jesus

A friend of mine, Stephen Dickie, describes meeting with a prominent Sheik in Australia one morning for breakfast. Over their meal they started discussing the commonalities between their two religions: Christianity as represented by Seventh-day Adventists and Islam. They started with their common spiritual heritage as children of Abraham. They followed the story of the collaboration between the descendants of Isaac and Ishmael (the Children of the East) all the way to Islam's role as a deliverer of God's people as predicted in the book of the Revelation of Jesus Christ.

The two men then moved on to their common beliefs: living a moral life, eating healthfully, avoiding stimulants and gambling, the role of the West in end time events, the state of the dead, Jesus' role on the Day of Judgment, etc. Finally, as they finished their mutually edifying conversation, the Sheik pulled back from the table, wiped his mouth with his napkin and broke the silence.

"It seems to me that you and I believe the same thing. What is it then that divides us?"

Stephen took a deep breath and plunged into what he knew was likely to be controversial and potentially could sever this newly formed friendship: "I think it's about Jesus..."

After nodding his head, the Sheik asked Stephen to explain himself. After his simple explanation, rather than abruptly ending the conversation, the Sheik invited him to come speak at his mosque. Something that over the centuries has divided the two great world religions had managed to bring two of their children together over that same subject.

This book will attempt to explain how that one great topic that has been the cause of so much misunderstanding, controversy and division over the years between Christians and Muslims: Jesus the Messiah (*Isa al-Masih*)—is really the one thing that can break down the walls, cross the divide and bridge the gap.

My theory is, like most problems of communication between different peoples, it's a matter of semantics: one person means one thing by one term and the other understands something completely different and thus communication has failed. And where communication fails, misunderstandings arise. And where misunderstandings arise eventually people start fighting and killing each other.

Part of the problem is when people of faith start thinking they have all the truth and have nothing more to learn. Christians say that all revelation ceased with the last words of the New Testament. Muslims say that all revelation ended with Muhammad and the Qur'an. Yet this goes against the actual teachings found in those books.

*Surely the Lord God will do nothing,*
*but he revealeth his secret*
*unto his servants the prophets.*

Amos 3:7 (KJV)

Unless God has ceased having any plans for His people since the Bible was finished about 2000 years ago, He must have been giving fresh revelations from time to time. So the Bible can't be the end of inspired revelation. God's plan throughout history has been progressive revelation, not final revelation. As Jesus himself said to his disciples on the eve of the end of his time on earth:

*I have yet many things to say unto you,*
*but ye cannot bear them now.*
*Howbeit when he, the Spirit of truth,*
*is come, he will guide you into all truth*

John 16:12-13 (KJV)

If those who were next to Jesus, saw all his miracles and heard all his teachings still had so much more to learn, how can we be so arrogant as to think that we have it all figured out? Jesus is very clear: it's God's Spirit speaking to believers throughout the ages that will little by little continue to bring truth into the world. The Qur'an says the same thing:

*Knower of the unseen,*
*He does not reveal His unseen to anyone.*
*Except to whom He has accepted as a messenger,*
*then He reveals from the past and the future.*
*So that He knows that they have*
*delivered the messages of their Lord,...*

Qur'an 72:26-28

*God guides to the truth...*
*This Qur'an could not have been produced without God:*
*it is to authenticate what is between his hands,*
*and to give details of the Book*
*in which there is no doubt from the Lord of the Worlds...*
*And for every nation there is a messenger;*
*so when their messenger comes,*
*the matter is decreed between them with justice...*

Qur'an 10:35,37,47

So the Qur'an confirms what the Bible says: only God brings truth and He reveals it so that we will understand the past and prepare for the future. For every nation, not just the ones in the past, God has sent, and will send, messages through His messengers.

So, let's attempt to set aside tradition and bias and see what the Qur'an and the Bible say about Jesus the Messiah (*Isa al-Masih*), praying for the Spirit of God to lead us into all truth.

# The Holy Books

*And as for Ishmael, I have heard thee:*
*Behold, I have blessed him,*
*and will make him fruitful,*
*and will multiply him exceedingly;*
*twelve princes shall he beget,*
*and I will make him a great nation.*

Genesis 17:20 (KJV)

*If you are in doubt regarding*
*what We have sent down to you,*
*then ask those who have been reading*
*the Book from before you.*
*The truth has come to you from your Lord,*
*so do not be of those who doubt.*

Qur'an 10:94

   In my previous book, *The Children of the East: the Spiritual Heritage of Islam in the Bible*, I traced the history of Ishmael and his descendants through the Old and New Testaments (*Tawrat, Zaboor,* and *Injeel*) and showed how the two sons of Abraham, Isaac and Ishmael always worked together to accomplish God's purposes. From Joseph and the Ishmaelite traders, to Moses and Jethro, to Caleb and Joshua, to Balaam and Job, to Deborah and Yael, to Jehu and Jonadab, to the Rechabites and the Wise Men from the East, to Saul (Paul) and the Nabataeans, all the way to the rise of Islam as predicted in the Revelation of Jesus Christ chapter nine; the Bible recognizes that the line of Ishmael, including Islam, has been used by God to accomplish His purposes. The conclusion is simple: if Islam was used by God, then it's holy book, the Qur'an, has also been used by God.

At the same time, the Qur'an mentions numerous times that the Holy Books that came before the Qur'an were also inspired, to be respected and to be used to clarify doubts. The following are only a sample of verses from the Qur'an showing the validity of the previous scriptures, what Christians call the Bible:

*And We gave Moses the Book,*
*and after him We sent the messengers.*
*And We gave Jesus, Son of Mary, the clear proofs,*
*and we supported him with the Holy Spirit...*

Qur'an 2:87

*He sent down to you the Book with the truth,*
*authenticating what is between his hands;*
*and He sent down the Torah and the Gospel*
*from before as a guidance for the people,*
*and He sent down the Criterion.*
*Those who rejected the revelations of God,*
*they will have a severe retribution...*

Qur'an 3:3-4

*If they deny you, then messengers before you were also denied;*
*they came with the proofs and the scriptures*
*and the Book of Enlightenment.*

Qur'an 3:184

*...We have instructed those who were given the Book before you,...*
*O you who believe; believe in God and His messenger,*
*and the Book which was sent down to His messenger,*
*and the Book which was sent before.*
*And whoever rejects God, and His angels,*
*and His Books, and His messengers, and the Last Day;*
*then he has strayed a far straying.*

Qur'an 4:131,136

*We have inspired you as We had inspired Noah*
*and the prophets after him.*
*And We had inspired Abraham, and Ishmael,*

*and Isaac, and Jacob, and the Patriarchs,*
*and Jesus, and Job, and Jonah,*
*and Aaron, and Solomon;*
*and We gave David the Psalms.*

Qur'an 4:163

*And We sent in their footsteps Jesus, Son of Mary,*
*authenticating what was present with him of the Torah.*
*And We gave him the Gospel,*
*in it is a guidance and a light,*
*and authenticating what was present with him of the Torah,*
*and a guidance and a lesson for the righteous.*

Qur'an 5:46

*"Who then has sent down the Book*
*which Moses had come with,*
*a light and a guidance for the people?...God has."*

Qur'an 6:91

*Then We gave Moses the Book,*
*to complete for those who do right,*
*and to fully detail all things,*
*and a guide and mercy*
*that they may believe in the meeting of their Lord.*

Qur'an 6:154

*God has purchased from the believers*
*their very lives and their wealth,*
*that they will have the Paradise...*
*a promise that is true upon Him*
*in the Torah and the Gospel and the Qur'an.*

Qur'an 9:111

*And We did not send any except men*
*before you whom We inspired,*
*so ask the people who have received the Reminder*
*if you do not know.*

*With proofs and the scriptures.*
*And We sent down to you the Reminder*
*to reveal to the people what was sent to them,*
*and perhaps they will think.*

Qur'an 16:43-44

*...And We have preferred*
*some prophets over others,*
*and We gave David the Psalms.*

Qur'an 17:55

*And We have written in the Psalms:*
*"After the remembrance,*
*that the earth will be inherited*
*by My servants who do good."*

Qur'an 21:105

*And this is a revelation from the Lord of the worlds.*
*It was sent down with the trusted Spirit.*
*Upon your heart, so that you would be of the warners.*
*In a clear Arabic tongue.*
*And it is in the scriptures of old.*
*Was it not a sign for them that the scholars*
*of the Children of Israel knew it?*

Qur'an 26:192-197

*There was not a nation that a warner did not come to it.*
*And if they deny you,*
*then those before them have also denied.*
*Their messengers went to them*
*with the proofs and the scriptures,*
*and the Book of Enlightenment.*

Qur'an 35:23-25

*And We gave Moses the guidance,*
*and We made the Children of Israel inherit the Book.*
*A guide and a reminder*

*for those who possess intelligence.*

Qur'an 40:53-54

*And before it was the Book of Moses,*
*a beacon and a mercy.*
*And this is an authenticating Book,*
*in an Arabic tongue,*
*so that you may warn those who have transgressed,*
*and to give good news to the righteous.*

Qur'an 46:12

*...Such is their example in the Torah.*
*And their example in the Gospel*
*is like a plant which shoots out*
*and becomes strong and thick*
*and it stands straight on its trunk,*
*pleasing to the farmers...*

Qur'an 48:29

*...Do any of you wish to learn?*
*And everything they had done, is in the scriptures.*
*And everything, small or large, is written down.*

Qur'an 54:51-53

These examples plus numerous others reveal that the Qur'an considered the Book (Bible)—specifically the Torah (*Tawrat*), the Psalms (*Zaboor*) and the Gospels (*Injeel*)—to be part of the same revelation consistent with, and clarifying, the messages in the Qur'an.

Many Muslims believe that those previous scriptures no longer exist in the original and have therefore become corrupted. However, history shows us that it is actually thanks to the Muslim scholars in Islamic libraries that the original Greek manuscripts pre-dating Islam were preserved.

At the time that Islam was arising, Europe was in the Dark Ages and Christians weren't copying any of the fragile Greek manuscripts (mostly written on papyrus) including the Old and New Testaments because they only wanted the scriptures to be in Latin. However, in the great libraries of the Islamic world, those ancient manuscripts were carefully preserved and copied to ensure that no changes were made to the originals (see http://en.wikipedia.org/wiki/Arab_transmission_of_the_Classics_to_the_ West).

In fact, the Qur'an itself doesn't give any indication that the Book that came before the Qur'an was corrupted but rather that the people of the Book (Jews and Christians) were twisting what their scriptures said and even lying about the Bible.

Unfortunately, this practice continues today in all religions who have been given scriptures; people take verses out of context and manipulate them to serve their own purposes. The following verses from the Qur'an are warnings to us all to carefully seek out truth and not listen to what human beings try to tell us the Holy Books are saying:

*"O people of the Book,*
*why do you debate with us regarding Abraham*
*when the Torah and the Gospel*
*were not sent down except after him?*
*Do you not comprehend?...*

*A group from the people of the Book*
*wished that they could misguide you,*
*but they only misguide themselves*
*and they do not notice.*
*O people of the Book,*
*why do you reject the revelations of God*
*while you are bearing witness?*
*O people of the Book,*
*why do you confound the truth with falsehood*
*and conceal the truth while you know?...*

*And from among them is a group*
*who twist their tongues with the Book*
*so that you may think it is from the Book,*
*while it is not from the Book,*
*and they say it is from God*
*while it is not from God,*
*and they say about God lies while they know...*

*Say: 'We believe in God*
*and what was sent down to us*
*and what was sent down to Abraham and Ishmael*
*and Isaac and Jacob and the Patriarchs,*

*and what was given to Moses and Jesus*
*and the prophets from their Lord.*
*We do not make a distinction between any of them,*
*and to Him we submit.'*

Qur'an 3:65-84

So let us put prejudice aside and recognize the sovereignty of God to reveal his messages to whomever He will. Let's try and sweep back tradition, superstition, and the ideas of men and look only at the Qur'an and the Gospels, and see what they can teach us about this Jesus who is so respected by both Christians and Muslims and yet the source of so much division and fighting. The journey is open to those who are willing to travel the road. As the famous Bedouin proverb says, "When you sleep in a house your thoughts are as high as the ceiling, when you sleep outside they are as high as the stars." Let's seek for truth. As Jesus says in the Gospels:

*"And ye shall know the truth,*
*and the truth shall make you free."*

John 8:32 (KJV)

## CONCLUSION

In conclusion, the Bible recognizes that truth is progressive and that it is only as we are ready that God's Spirit leads us into more and more truth. The Qur'an also recognizes the previous scriptures revealed by God, including those given to Moses (the Torah), David (the Psalms) and Jesus (the Gospels). Therefore, there should be no contradiction between all the inspired Holy Books and any apparent contradictions are simply misunderstanding on the readers part that should be resolved with study, prayer and the leading of God's Spirit.

# One God

*Hear, O Israel: The Lord our God is one Lord*

Deuteronomy 6:4 (KJV)

*Now an intermediary implies more than one,
but God is one.*

Galatians 3:20 (ESV)

*You believe that God is one; you do well.
Even the demons believe—and shudder!*

James 2:19 (ESV)

*Say "He is God, the One,
God the Indivisible
He does not beget nor was He begotten
And there is none who is His equal."*

Qur'an 112

*Your God is indeed One.*

Qur'an 37:4

One day a scribe comes to Jesus and asks him an important question: "Which commandment is the most important of all?"

Jesus turns, looks the man in the eye, and quotes the Torah: "Hear, O Israel, the Lord our God, is one Lord" (Deuteronomy 6:4 KJV).

Seeing the wisdom of Jesus' reply, the scribe says, "You are right, Teacher. You have truly said that he is one, and there is no other besides him." (see Mark 12:28-32).

The Bible is clear. Both the Torah (*Tawrat*) and the Gospels (*Injeel*) state as of primary importance in religion the belief that God is the one and only. The Jews call this the *Shema* (testimony or witness). The Muslims call it the *Shahada* (testimony or witness): there is no God except the God (*la ilah ila Al-Lah*)

This is the foundation of monotheism, including Christianity and Islam. Yet each religion claims that the other one is blasphemous. How did this happen? Misunderstanding, traditions, arguments, disputes, superiority complexes, ignorance, unforgiving spirits, pride, selfishness, wars, lust for power, manipulation, fear, coercion and close-mindedness have all played a role. Certainly the Gospels are clear that there is only one God and rejects polytheism:

> *...We know that an idol is nothing in the world,*
> *and that there is none other God but one.*
> *For though there be that are called gods,*
> *whether in heaven or in earth,*
> *(as there be gods many, and lords many,)*
> *But to us there is but one God, the Father,*
> *of whom are all things, and we in him;*
> *and one Lord Jesus Christ,*
> *by whom are all things, and we by him.*

1 Corinthians 8:4-6 (KJV)

Christians believe in One God, the Creator who they call Father because He has made all things and cares for all His creation. Unfortunately, it's come to the point that many Christians feel that Allah and God are different gods. There are many reasons, however, to believe that they are the same. Several other books have been written on the subject in depth (including *Allah: a Christian Perspective* by Miroslav Volf).

Briefly, though, it's clear that Allah and God are the same as they both claim to be the God of Adam, Noah, Abraham, Isaac, Jacob, Jesus and the other prophets. The Qur'an is clear that the God of the Christians and Jews (people of the Book) is the same as the Muslim Allah:

> *And do not argue with the people of the Book*
> *except in that which is better;*

*except for those who are wicked among them:*
*and say: "We believe in what was revealed to us*
*and in what was revealed to you,*
*and our god and your god is the same;*
*to Him we submit."*

Qur'an 29:46

*Al-Lah* is not a name for a god, but the actual word in the Arabic language meaning "the God." Since the time of Pentecost (Acts 2:11) Arab Christians have been calling the Creator, Allah, and every Arabic Bible refers to Him by this name.

This is the basis for our journey towards the discovery of who Jesus is. The same God is the God of both Islam and Christianity, the Qur'an and the Gospels. Hard and difficult as it may seem to our limited understanding of a limitless God, the premise still is true that God is beyond anything that we can even begin to comprehend.

## CONCLUSION

In conclusion, Christians and Muslims both have as their foundation the worship of One God and that One God is the same no matter what language one uses to name Him. Both religions worship the God who created the heavens and the earth and who is the God of Adam, Noah, Abraham, Moses, David, and Jesus. Anything that seems contrary to that must therefore be a misunderstanding or something based on tradition rather than scripture.

# Son of Mary

*...We sent her Our spirit,*
*which appeared to her just like a man...*
*He said, "I am only a messenger from your Lord,*
*to give you a sinless son...*
*That was Jesus, Son of Mary*
*A word of truth about which they doubt.*

Qur'an 19:17, 19, 34

*And Mary said to the angel,*
*"How will this be, since I am a virgin?"*
*And the angel answered her,*
*"The Holy Spirit will come upon you,*
*and the power of the Most High will overshadow you;*
*therefore the child to be born will be called holy...*
*For nothing will be impossible with God."*

Luke 1:34-37 (ESV)

*She said, "My Lord! How can I have a son,*
*When no man has touched me?..."*
*Thus does God create at will:*
*When God decides on something,*
*God simply says to it 'Be!' and it is.*

Qur'an 3:45-47

The discussion of Jesus in the Qur'an and the Gospels must necessarily begin with his birth, especially since that birth is surrounded by mysterious circumstances. Both the Qur'an and the Gospels not only each mention the virgin birth of Jesus, the Son of Mary, but each refers to that event twice and each does it slightly differently each time. Here is the first story of Jesus' birth in the Qur'an:

*And the angels said, "O Mary,*
*God has chosen you and purified you,*
*chosen you over the women of all peoples,*
*Mary, obey your lord devoutly,*
*worship, and bow in prayer*
*with those bowing in prayer."*
*That is from communications of the unseen,*
*which We intimate to you.*
*You were not with them*
*when they were casting lots to decide*
*which of them would support Mary,*
*and you were not with them*
*when they were arguing.*
*The angels said,*
*"O Mary, God gives you good news*
*of a word from God,*
*named the Messiah,*
*Jesus Son of Mary,*
*honored in the world and the hereafter,*
*and one of the intimates of God.*
*And he will speak to the people*
*in infancy and maturity,*
*and be one of the righteous."*
*She said, "My Lord!*
*How can I have a son,*
*when no man has touched me?"*
*"Thus does God create at will:*
*when God decides on something,*
*God simply says to it 'Be!'*
*and it is."*

Qur'an 3:42-47

This passage brings out several important points. First of all, it was God's sovereign choice that Mary be the mother of Jesus. He could have chosen any number of women in whom to create this miraculous pregnancy, but He chose Mary.

Secondly, Mary's only claim to purity was through God since it was He who purified her. She didn't have her own righteousness; it came from God. However, even though God made her righteous, she still had a role to play. She needed to chose to obey, to humble herself, and to pray.

These verses also indicate that Jesus' birth was part of a plan formulated in the spiritual world: "communications from the unseen." This birth was something specially engineered by God through His Spirit and with the help of the angels long before the virgin became pregnant.

The Qur'an also reports that this pregnancy was a miracle. Mary had never had sexual relations, the normal way of getting pregnant for women throughout history. Rather, she states that "no man has touched me." Then God goes on to explain that her pregnancy will be an act of creation on the part of God using his word "Be! and it is" (*kun faya kun*).

Finally, the Qur'an states that the child to be born of this miraculous creation in the uterus of a virgin will be someone special. Jesus is a "word from God" (*Kalimat Allah*), "the Messiah" (*al-Masih*), "honored in the world and the hereafter," "one of the intimates of God," and "one of the righteous."

Now let's look at the first mention of Jesus' birth in the Gospels:

> *Now the birth of Jesus Christ took place in this way.*
> *When his mother Mary had been betrothed to Joseph,*
> *before they came together she was found*
> *to be with child from the Holy Spirit.*
> *And her husband Joseph, being a just man*
> *and unwilling to put her to shame,*
> *resolved to divorce her quietly.*
> *But as he considered these things,*
> *behold, an angel of the Lord*
> *appeared to him in a dream, saying,*
> *"Joseph, son of David, do not fear to take Mary as your wife,*
> *for that which is conceived in her is from the Holy Spirit.*
> *She will bear a son, and you shall call his name Jesus,*
> *for he will save his people from their sins."*
> *All this took place to fulfill*
> *what the Lord had spoken by the prophet:*
> *"Behold, the virgin shall conceive and bear a son,*
> *and they shall call his name Immanuel"*
> *(which means, God with us).*
> *When Joseph woke from his sleep,*
> *he did as the angel of the Lord commanded him:*
> *he took his wife,*

*but knew her not until she had given birth to a son.*
*And he called his name Jesus.*

Matthew 1:18-25 (ESV)

These verses of scripture repeat several of the things found in the first story in the Qur'an: Mary was a virgin when she became pregnant with Jesus, the pregnancy was a miracle from God through His Spirit, angels were involved in the communication of this event, this intervention from God was planned in advance since it would "fulfill what the Lord had spoken through the prophet," and the Son of Mary was to be someone special who would "save his people from their sins."

This passage also introduces the man who would be the adopted—not biological—father of Jesus: Joseph. It's clear that Joseph had nothing to do with the pregnancy which would result in the birth of the Messiah. He did not have relations with Mary until Jesus was born. However, he would play the role of father in the early life of Jesus, helping him to get to know God and teaching him the way of all believers.

Now let's look at the second passage concerning the Messiah's birth in the Qur'an:

*And relate in the Book, Mary,*
*when she withdrew herself from her family*
*to a place which was to the east.*
*So she took a barrier to separate her from them,*
*so We sent Our Spirit to her,*
*and he took on the shape of a human being*
*in all similarity.*
*She said: "I seek refuge with the Almighty*
*from you if you are righteous."*
*He said: "I am the messenger of your Lord,*
*to grant you the gift of a pure son."*
*She said: "How can I have a son*
*when no human being has been with me,*
*nor have I desired such?"*
*He said: "It is such that your Lord has said,*
*it is easy for Me.*
*And We shall make him a sign for the people*
*and a mercy from Us.*
*It is a matter already ordained."*
*So she was pregnant with him,*
*and she went to deliver in a far place.*
*Then the birth pains came to her,*

*by the trunk of a palm tree.*
*She said: "I wish I had died before this,*
*and became totally forgotten!"*

Qur'an 19:16-23

This time, in the Qur'an we see that the Spirit of God (*Ruh Al-Lah*) is involved in the miraculous birth of Jesus as well as restating that it is a virgin birth. Once again we see that it was "a matter already ordained." In other words, God has been planning this birth and has a special role for this child: he will be "a sign for the people and a mercy" from God.

These verses also introduce two more important characteristics of the Son of Mary: he is a gift and he is pure. The first person to benefit from this gift is Jesus' mother. Jesus is given to her as a miracle directly from God for whom this gift of a pure son "is easy." But then the gift of the sinlessly pure life of this child is extended to all humanity: "We shall make him a sign for the people and a mercy from Us."

The Qur'an also makes clear that after the miraculous conception of Jesus, the pregnancy and birth were normal, like women throughout time have had. When "the birth pains came to" Mary she cries out in agony, "I wish I had died before this, and become totally forgotten." This birth in the midst of pain and suffering prefigures the life of Jesus before he is taken up to God at the end of his earthly existence.

The Gospels also have a second story of the birth of the Son of Mary:

*In the sixth month the angel Gabriel*
*was sent from God*
*to a city of Galilee named Nazareth,*
*to a virgin betrothed to a man*
*whose name was Joseph,*
*of the house of David.*
*And the virgin's name was Mary.*
*And he came to her and said,*
*"Greetings, O favored one, the Lord is with you!"*
*But she was greatly troubled at the saying,*
*and tried to discern*
*what sort of greeting this might be.*
*And the angel said to her,*
*"Do not be afraid, Mary,*
*for you have found favor with God.*
*And behold, you will conceive*
*in your womb and bear a son,*

*and you shall call his name Jesus.*
*He will be great and will be called*
*the Son of the Most High.*
*And the Lord God will give to him*
*the throne of his father David,*
*and he will reign over the house of Jacob forever,*
*and of his kingdom there will be no end."*
*And Mary said to the angel,*
*"How will this be, since I am a virgin?"*
*And the angel answered her,*
*"The Holy Spirit will come upon you,*
*and the power of the Most High will overshadow you;*
*therefore the child to be born*
*will be called holy—the Son of God.*
*And behold, your relative Elizabeth in her old age*
*has also conceived a son,*
*and this is the sixth month*
*with her who was called barren.*
*For nothing will be impossible with God."*
*And Mary said, "Behold, I am the servant of the Lord;*
*let it be to me according to your word."*
*And the angel departed from her.*

Luke 1:26-38 (ESV)

This passage identifies the angel who came to Mary as none other than Gabriel himself; the same angel that would later appear to Muhammad in a cave outside Mecca. Just as in Qur'an 19, Mary is afraid of the angel when she first encounters him but is soon reassured that he has come with Good News: she has found favor with God and God has something very special in store for her.

Again the virginity of Mary is reinforced twice in verse 27 and later by Mary herself in verse 34. This was no ordinary birth, but a miracle of God: "For nothing will be impossible with God." Mary then submits to the will of God and humbly accepts her role as mother of this special child.

The direct creation by God of this miracle in the virgin Mary's womb in verse 35 uses the same language that the Torah uses to describe the creation of the world, including the first man, Adam:

*In the beginning,*
*God created the heaven and the earth.*
*The earth was without form, and void;*

*and darkness was upon the face of the deep.*
*And the Spirit of God moved*
*upon the face of the waters...*
*And God said, Let us make man*
*in our image, after our likeness...*

Genesis 1:1-2,26 (KJV)

The Qur'an also compares the conception of Jesus to that of the creation of Adam:

*The example of Jesus with God*
*is similar to that of Adam;*
*He created him from dust,*
*then He said to him "Be" and he was.*

Qur'an 3:59

The Gospel narrative also brings up a controversial point that will be dealt with more in detail in a later chapter. However, it is necessary to touch on that here in order to help clarify a potential misunderstanding. Luke 1:32 and 35 states that Jesus will be called "Son of the Most High" and "the Son of God."

The idea that God would have a son by the human route of procreation is blasphemous to both Muslims and Christians. And these verses make clear that the title "Son of God" doesn't mean a literal son, but rather a figurative one. For example, Luke 1:32 also says that Jesus' father is David. Jesus can't be both the literal son of God and the son of David therefore the logical conclusion is that he is neither the biological son of David nor the biological son of God. Instead, the terms "son" and "father" are figurative bringing out the idea that the Son of Mary is the one to fulfill the promises made by God to David of a Messiah, a special anointed one who will by called "pure" (Qur'an 19:19) and "holy" (Luke 1:35).

Also, coming back to the comparison of Jesus and Adam the same Gospel that calls Jesus the "Son of God" (Luke 1:35) also calls Adam "the Son of God" (Luke 3:38). Adam's being called the Son of God doesn't mean God was his literal father, but rather his Creator. Therefore, Jesus' being called the Son of God by Gabriel—right after using the same language as used in the Genesis creation account—also was in relation to the miraculous creation in Mary's womb simply by the powerful word of God, "Be!" Therefore, the literal Son of Mary also becomes the figurative Son of God through the miracle of the virgin birth.

These four versions of the miraculous virgin birth of the Son of Mary, two in the Gospels and two in the Qur'an, alone should be enough to quell any disputes about Jesus among Christians and Muslims. The fact that the conception and birth of Jesus are described in exactly the same way not once but twice in each Scripture means that no matter what each religion may dispute about the Son of Mary's later life, since Jesus' beginning is the same in both religions, then Jesus has to be the same in both religions. Jesus didn't suddenly change and become something different after his conception and birth. What Jesus is was determined from the moment God performed the miracle through the Holy Spirit to place him in the womb of the virgin Mary.

Instead of fighting among themselves, could it be that both Christians and Muslims were meant to learn from each other about God and about Jesus? As the Qur'an says:

*O people of the Book,*
*let us come to a common understanding*
*between us and between you;*
*that we serve none except God,*
*and that we do not set up anything with Him,*
*and that none of us takes*
*each other as patrons besides God.*

Qur'an 3:64

*And do not argue with the people of the Book*
*except in that which is better...and say:*
*"We believe in what was revealed to us*
*and in what was revealed to you,*
*and our God and your God is the same;*
*to Him we submit."*

Qur'an 29:46

## CONCLUSION

In conclusion, the Jesus of the Qur'an and the Gospels was conceived in the womb of a virgin by a direct, miraculous intervention of God through His Spirit and as a result, the Son of Mary would be someone unusually important: pure, holy, a sign and a mercy from God first to his mother and then to all of humanity.

Also, "Son of God", is not a literal term but a figurative one. Jesus is called both Son of God and Son of David even though the same passage relates that his mother was a virgin. Therefore, he couldn't be the literal son of either. Jesus is compared to Adam as well in the Qur'an and the Gospels and both are called the "Son of God" because they both were directly created by God rather than being the product of normal human procreation.

Finally, the Jesus of the Qur'an and the Gospels is the same because the story of the origin of his earthly life is identical in both Scriptures.

# Servant

*The Messiah is not too proud*
*to be a servant to God,*
*nor are the angels*
*who are close to Him.*

Qur'an 4:172

*...Christ Jesus...made himself of no reputation,*
*and took upon him the form of a servant,*
*and was made in the likeness of men:*
*And being found in fashion as a man,*
*he humbled himself,*
*and became obedient...*

Philippians 2:5,7-8 (NIV)

One of the favorite titles in the Qur'an for God's friends, messengers, prophets and people is "servant of God" (*abd Allah*). In fact, this name, Abdallah, has been taken by many Muslims throughout the centuries. It is the perfect name for a Muslim, one who submits to God. What better way of expressing one's submission to the greatness of God than to humble ourselves and take on the title of "servant" or "slave" of God.

So despite the fact that Jesus is called the Messiah, a Spirit from God, pure, a Word from God, a prophet, and does many extraordinary things like healing the blind and lepers and raising the dead, despite all this, Jesus expresses humility in the face of God by calling himself a "servant."

*He [Jesus] said: "I am a servant of God,*
*He has given me the book*
*and made me a prophet.*

*And He has made me blessed wherever I am..."*

Qur'an 19:30-31

The paradox which characterizes so much about God is that by humbling ourselves we are lifted up; by submitting ourselves to God we become blessed. So in the Qur'an, Jesus is held out as an example of those who humble themselves and submit (Muslims) and as one who can help clarify the things that people dispute about if we obey him.

*And when the Son of Mary was put forth as an example,*
*your people turned away from it...*
*He was no more than a servant whom We blessed,*
*and we made him an example for the Children of Israel...*
*And he was a lesson for the Hour.*
*So have no doubt about it.*
*And follow Me; this is a straight path...*
*And when Jesus came with the proofs, he said:*
*"I have come to you with the wisdom,*
*and to clarify some of the matters in which you dispute.*
*So be aware of God and obey me."*

Qur'an 43:57-63

In the gospels, despite the fame that his miracles bring him, Jesus is not afraid to humble himself and continually submit to God's will. Right at the end of his earthly mission, Jesus meets one last time with his disciples to eat a meal in celebration of the Jewish Passover feast.

*Now before the feast of the passover,*
*when Jesus knew that his hour was come*
*that he should depart out of this world unto the Father,*
*having loved his own which were in the world,*
*he loved them unto the end.*
*And supper being ended,*
*the devil having now put into the heart*
*of Judas Iscariot, Simon's son, to betray him;*
*Jesus knowing that the Father*
*had given all things into his hands,*
*and that he was come from God, and went to God;*
*He riseth from supper, and laid aside his garments;*
*and took a towel, and girded himself.*

*After that he poureth water into a basin,*
*and began to wash the disciples' feet,*
*and to wipe them with the towel wherewith he was girded.*

John 13:1-5 (KJV)

In those days, only the lowest of servants washed the feet of guests. Walking in sandals on Palestine's dusty roads made for dirty, stinky feet at the end of the day. No one but the most lowly of slaves would ever be required to perform such a lowly task. But at this feast, there was no servant, so Jesus' disciples were all mumbling among themselves as to who should do the necessary task of washing the others' feet. Each felt that one of the others should do it, certainly not him!

So Jesus showed that he is not too proud or arrogant to be a servant, even though he was their leader and the Messiah. He got down and washed their feet himself. If even a Messenger as great as Jesus could be a servant, how much more should we bow to God and serve his people with all our hearts and lives. Humbleness is what pleases God, while pride is dangerous. As the Bible (*Zaboor)* says:

*Pride goeth before destruction,*
*And an haughty spirit before a fall.*

Proverbs 16:18 (KJV)

After washing his disciples' feet, Jesus gave them his final message from God. Then he took his disciples out to an olive grove called the Garden of Gethsemane. There, Jesus fell on his face in prayer before God begging to not have to go through the suffering and death that God had warned him was part of His plan for him:

*And they schemed and God schemed,*
*but God is the best schemer.*
*For God said: "O Jesus, I will terminate your life,*
*and raise you to Me...*

Qur'an 3:44-45

In the end, though, Jesus submitted to God's will, demonstrating that he "is not too proud to be a servant to God" (Qur'an 4:172).

*And he [Jesus] said, Abba, Father,*

*all things are possible unto thee;*
*take away this cup from me:*
*nevertheless not what I will, but what thou wilt.*

Mark 14:36 (KJV)

## **<u>CONCLUSION</u>**

In conclusion, the Jesus of the Qur'an and the Gospels is a servant both to God and to his fellow human beings. He is not too proud to submit to God and to his brothers. He is an example to all believers of the attitude we should have towards our Creator and our fellow man.

# Healer

*...and I [Jesus] heal the blind and the lepers,*
*and give life to the dead*
*with the permission of God,...*

Qur'an 3:49

*"...and you [Jesus] would heal the blind and the leper*
*with My permission..."*

Qur'an 5:110

*And great multitudes came unto him,*
*having with them those that were*
*lame, blind, dumb, maimed, and many others,*
*and cast them down at Jesus' feet;*
*and he healed them:*

Matthew 15:30 (KJV)

While the Qur'an mentions only in passing that Jesus healed the sick, the Gospels go into great detail and spend much of their time telling the stories of times when Jesus healed the sick and cast out demons. Here are a few of the many stories the Gospels relate about Jesus' ability to heal the sick.

*And, behold, there came a leper*
*and worshipped him, saying,*
*Lord, if thou wilt,*
*thou canst make me clean.*
*And Jesus put forth his hand,*
*and touched him, saying,*

*I will; be thou clean.*
*And immediately his leprosy was cleansed.*

Matthew 8:2-3 (KJV)

*And as he entered into a certain village*
*there met him ten men that were lepers,*
*which stood afar off:*
*And they lifted up their voices, and said,*
*Jesus, Master, have mercy on us.*
*And when he saw them, he said unto them,*
*Go shew yourselves unto the priests.*
*And it came to pass, that,*
*as they went, they were cleansed.*
*And one of them, when he saw that he was healed,*
*turned back, and with a loud voice glorified God,*
*And fell down on his face at his feet,*
*giving him thanks: and he was a Samaritan.*
*And Jesus answering said,*
*Were there not ten cleansed? but where are the nine?*
*There are not found that returned*
*to give glory to God, save this stranger.*
*And he said unto him, Arise, go thy way:*
*thy faith hath made thee whole.*

Luke 17:12-19 (KJV)

Jesus healed the lepers because he was moved with compassion and wanted to heal them. And Jesus knew the power of God and so wasn't afraid to touch them. They stood at a distance because leprosy was so feared in those days because of its contagious nature that lepers were not allowed to approach non lepers without crying out "Unclean! Unclean! Impure! Impure!" Jesus knew that by God's permission he had the power to heal so he reached out and touched them. Contrary to normal means of disease transmission where the sick contaminate the well, when Jesus touched the lepers he wasn't contaminated but rather it is they who were cleansed, made pure, and healed.

These verses also teach us that after we have benefitted from a miracle of God, we should be grateful and give God the praise that is due Him. Only one of the ten lepers came back praising God. And it was a foreigner, one that was despised by the Jews of Jesus' time. God does not favor any one but has compassion on all who have faith no matter what language, tribe, people or culture. And because of his gratitude and giving thanks to God, this one former leper also received a blessing that the others missed out on.

*And they came to Jericho:*
*and as he went out of Jericho*
*with his disciples and a great number of people,*
*blind Bartimaeus, the son of Timaeus,*
*sat by the highway side begging.*
*And when he heard that it was Jesus of Nazareth,*
*he began to cry out, and say,*
*Jesus, thou Son of David, have mercy on me.*
*And many charged him that he should hold his peace:*
*but he cried the more a great deal,*
*Thou Son of David, have mercy on me.*
*And Jesus stood still, and commanded him to be called.*
*And they call the blind man, saying unto him,*
*Be of good comfort, rise; he calleth thee.*
*And he, casting away his garment,*
*rose, and came to Jesus.*
*And Jesus answered and said unto him,*
*What wilt thou that I should do unto thee?*
*The blind man said unto him,*
*Lord, that I might receive my sight.*
*And Jesus said unto him,*
*Go thy way; thy faith hath made thee whole.*
*And immediately he received his sight,*
*and followed Jesus in the way.*

Mark 10:46-52 (KJV)

*...and they bring a blind man unto him [Jesus],*
*and besought him to touch him.*
*And he took the blind man by the hand,*
*and led him out of the town;*
*and when he had spit on his eyes,*
*and put his hands upon him,*
*he asked him if he saw ought.*
*And he looked up, and said,*
*I see men as trees, walking.*
*After that he put his hands again upon his eyes,*
*and made him look up:*

39

*and he was restored,*
*and saw every man clearly.*

Mark 8:22-25 (KJV)

Jesus could never refuse someone who begged for healing. Sometimes, he used just a word and healing was instantaneous. Sometimes, he used local remedies and it was a process. But, no one who came looking for healing left without getting what they were searching for. Jesus never refused to heal anyone who had faith. Jesus was given power by God to heal not only the lepers and the blind but to cast out evil spirits who were tormenting people.

*Then was brought unto him one possessed*
*with a devil, blind, and dumb:*
*and he healed him, insomuch that*
*the blind and dumb both spake and saw.*
*And all the people were amazed, and said,*
*Is not this the Son of David?*

Matthew 12:22-23 (KJV)

*And, behold, a woman of Canaan*
*came out of the same coasts,*
*and cried unto him, saying,*
*Have mercy on me, O Lord, thou Son of David;*
*my daughter is grievously vexed with a devil..*
*Then Jesus answered and said unto her,*
*O woman, great is thy faith:*
*be it unto thee even as thou wilt.*
*And her daughter was made whole from that very hour.*

Matthew 15:22, 28 (KJV)

As we can see, the Son of Mary was given extraordinary powers from God. We also can see that he is called the Son of David even though obviously he was not the literal "son" of the ancient Jewish king since both the Gospels and the Qur'an state that Jesus had no earthly father, but was rather the miraculous creation by God of a pregnancy in the womb of a virgin named Mary. In the next chapter we'll find out what the term "Son of David" meant to those using this term for Jesus.

## <u>CONCLUSION</u>

In conclusion, the Jesus of the Qur'an and the Gospels had power to heal the sick and chase out demons with a single word, even though at times he used local remedies. This power came to him from God who is the only one with that kind of power. And Jesus used that power often because he had compassion and love for those who were suffering. Finally, whenever we benefit from a direct intervention on God's part we should be grateful and give Him all the praise.

# Messiah

*And the angels said:*
*"O Mary, God gives you glad tidings*
*of a word from Him.*
*His name is the Messiah,*
*Jesus, Son of Mary.*
*Honorable in this world*
*and the Hereafter,*
*and from among those who are made close.*

Qur'an 3:45

*...and Jacob the father of Joseph*
*the husband of Mary,*
*and Mary was the mother of Jesus*
*who is called the Messiah.*

Luke 20:41-44 (NIV)

Messiah is a Hebrew word, משיח (pronounced *mashiah*), meaning "anointed one" and is used for many kings and priests in the Torah (*Tawrat*) and the Psalms (*Zaboor*). In the Gospels, which were written in Greek, Χριστός (pronounced *khristos'*) is used which is transliterated into the English, Christ. In the Qur'an, the word in Arabic, المسيح (pronounced *al-Masih),* is similar to the word in Hebrew since they are sister languages. In the Gospels and the Qur'an, Messiah is used uniquely in reference to Jesus, the Son of Mary.

In the Qur'an, Jesus is called the Messiah 11 times.

*...O Mary, God gives you glad tidings*
*of a word from Him.*

*His name is the Messiah,*
*Jesus, Son of Mary...*

Qur'an 3:45

*And their saying: "We have killed*
*the Messiah, Jesus, Son of Mary,*
*messenger of God!"...*

Qur'an 4:157

*...[The Messiah], Jesus, Son of Mary,*
*was no more than a messenger of God*
*and the fulfillment of His word to Mary*
*and a Spirit from Him...*
*The Messiah is not too proud*
*to be a servant to God...*

Qur'an 4:171-172

*Rejecters indeed are those who have said:*
*"God is the Messiah, Son of Mary."*
*Say: "Who has any power against God*
*if He had wanted to destroy the Messiah,*
*Son of Mary, and his mother,*
*and all who are on the earth!"...*

Qur'an 5:17

*Rejecters indeed are those who have said:*
*"God is the Messiah, Son of Mary."*
*And the Messiah said: "O Children of Israel,*
*serve God, my Lord and your Lord...*
*The Messiah Son of Mary*
*is no more than a messenger..."*

Qur'an 5:72, 75

*The Jews said: "Ezra is the son of God,"*
*and the Nazarenes said "The Messiah is the son of God..."*
*They have taken their Priests and Monks*
*to be patrons besides God,*

*and the Messiah, Son of Mary,*
*while they were only commanded to serve One god,*
*there is no god except He...*

Qur'an 9:30-31

The Qur'an is clear that God is not the Messiah, the Messiah is not the son of God and he is not to be taken as a patron other than God. It says that the Messiah is a messenger and that he is a servant of God who is his Lord. However, the Qur'an also states that while the Messiah is no more than a messenger he is also a subject of glad tidings (*bashshir*), a word from God (*kalimata minhu*), His word to Mary (*kalimatuhu al qahaila maryam*), and a Spirit from Him (*ruhun minhu*). So while the Messiah is "no more than a messenger," he is a special one.

But doesn't this contradict the Gospels? Don't they say that God is the Messiah? Actually, it's subtle, but they don't say that God is the Messiah. However, they do say the following:

*For in Christ all the fullness of the Deity*
*lives in bodily form.*

Colossians 2:9 (NIV)

In other words, the Messiah is the bodily representation of the fullness of God's character (His Spirit and Word) as much as the infinite God could be portrayed in a three dimensional world. This is the mystery of Jesus that has been debated by theologians throughout the centuries: the combination of the human and the divine.

The Gospels mention "Messiah" 50 times and "Christ" four times (two times it is to clarify that Christ means Messiah). As was mentioned earlier, Messiah means "anointed one" in Hebrew, Greek (Christ) and Arabic (*al-Masih*). It was a term used for one that was anointed with oil which was a symbol of being set apart for a special mission from God, usually a prophet, a priest or a king.

Messiah also came to be used by the Jews as a symbol of one who would come from the descendants of King David (hence the term "Son of David") and would bring freedom to Israel. In the Gospels, "Son of David" and "Messiah" were used interchangeably by the Jews. In fact, the first verse of the Gospels states:

*This is the genealogy of Jesus*
*the Messiah*

*the son of David*
*the son of Abraham*

Matthew 1:1 (NIV)

We've seen in previous chapters that several people, their hope fixed on the coming Messiah, called Jesus, "Son of David." The teachings from the Old Testament (*Tawrat* and *Zaboor*) on the Son of David and the Messiah were so ubiquitous that even the common people like the blind men and the Canaanite woman were familiar with them. In fact, the coming of the Son of David, or Messiah, was predicted hundreds of years before by the prophet Daniel:

> *Know therefore and understand,*
> *that from the going forth of the commandment*
> *to restore and to build Jerusalem*
> *unto the Messiah the Prince shall be seven weeks,*
> *and threescore and two weeks...*
> *And after threescore and two weeks*
> *shall Messiah be cut off, but not for himself...*

Daniel 9:25-26 (KJV)

In my previous book, *Children of the East: the Spiritual Heritage of Islam in the Bible*, I showed how the wise men (or magi) who came to celebrate Jesus' birth were Arabs, descendants of Ishmael, who had studied the prophecies of Daniel 9 (see above) and Balaam as recorded in the Torah (*Tawrat*):

> *I shall see him, but not now:*
> *I shall behold him, but not nigh:*
> *there shall come a Star out of Jacob,*
> *and a Sceptre shall rise out of Israel...*

Numbers 24:17 (KJV)

By following these prophecies, the Arab wise men knew that the Messiah was about to be born and when they saw a new star in the sky, they knew from Balaam's prophecy that they should follow it. First, the star led them to Jerusalem where they asked if anyone knew where they could find the Messiah, the newborn king.

*Magi from the east came to Jerusalem and asked,*
*"Where is the one who has been born king of the Jews?*
*We saw his star when it rose and have come to worship him."*
*When King Herod heard this he was disturbed,*
*and all Jerusalem with him.*
*When he had called together*
*all the people's chief priests and teachers of the law,*
*he asked them where the Messiah was to be born.*
*"In Bethlehem in Judea," they replied,*
*"for this is what the prophet has written:*
*'But you, Bethlehem, in the land of Judah,*
*are by no means least among the rulers of Judah;*
*for out of you will come a ruler*
*who will shepherd my people Israel.'"*

Matthew 2:1-6 (NIV)

The religious leaders recognized that the time was right for the Messiah to be born and they knew where the prophecies said he would be born: Bethlehem, the city of David the king. So the Arabs followed the star from Jerusalem and it led them directly the the house where Jesus the Messiah had just been born to the virgin Mary.

Jesus himself, when before the Roman Governor Pilate, explains that the idea of being the Messiah is not being an earthly king as the Jews expected, but that it was rather a spiritual kingdom.

*Then Pilate entered into the judgment hall again,*
*and called Jesus, and said unto him,*
*Art thou the King of the Jews?*

*Jesus answered him,*
*Sayest thou this thing of thyself,*
*or did others tell it thee of me?*

*Pilate answered,*
*Am I a Jew?*
*Thine own nation and the chief priests*
*have delivered thee unto me:*
*what hast thou done?*

*Jesus answered,*
*My kingdom is not of this world:*

*if my kingdom were of this world,*
*then would my servants fight,*
*that I should not be delivered to the Jews:*
*but now is my kingdom not from hence.*

*Pilate therefore said unto him,*
*Art thou a king then?*

*Jesus answered,*
*Thou sayest that I am a king.*
*To this end was I born,*
*and for this cause came I into the world,*
*that I should bear witness unto the truth.*
*Every one that is of the truth heareth my voice.*

John 18:33-37 (KJV)

So, being called the Messiah in both the Qur'an and the Bible give Jesus a unique distinction as one anointed by God for a special purpose; bring in a spiritual kingdom and testify to the truth about God. The other terms used in the Gospels to refer to the Messiah (Son of David, Son of God and Son of Man) are synonyms used to convey the specialness of this one anointed by God with a unique mission.

## CONCLUSION

In conclusion, the Jesus of the Qur'an and the Gospels is called the Messiah and in both it is a special designation setting him apart for a unique work that God called him to do: establish a spiritual kingdom on earth. While God is not the Messiah, the Messiah is the three-dimensional representation of the fulness of God in bodily form which is difficult to understand because it is part of the mystery of the infinite God who can do whatever He wants.

# Son of Man

*For God so loved the world,*
*that he gave his only begotten son,*
*that whosoever believeth in him should not perish,*
*but have everlasting life.*

John 3:16 (KJV)

*Say: "He is God, the One,*
*God, the Indivisible,*
*He does not beget, nor was He begotten,*
*And there is none who is His equal."*

Qur'an 112

Here we have the most popular verse in the Gospels, John 3:16, in apparent direct conflict with one of the most popular chapters in the Qur'an, quoted by most Muslims every day. Can there possibly be a way to reconcile this obvious contradiction between the two Holy Books?

Most misunderstandings are a result of miscommunication. One person says something which in his mind means one thing, but the other party understands a completely different thing from the phrase used.

A common example is the English word "gay". In today's world if I said, "he's gay" everyone would understand that I mean "he's a homosexual." However, a hundred years ago, the word "gay" meant "happy". For example, the popular Christmas song "Deck the Halls" says in one verse "Don we now our gay apparel" which didn't mean homosexual attire; it meant happy or festive clothes.

So words and meanings change and the important thing is that what the person speaking means is comprehended by the listener in exactly the same manner. So we need to have a closer look at this apparent contradiction between what the Bible says about Jesus and what the Qur'an says about him. First, let's look at the three verses in the Qur'an that directly relate to Jesus and the idea of "Son of God."

*Such was Jesus, Son of Mary,*
*and this is the truth of the matter in which they doubt.*
*God was never to take a son, be He glorified.*
*If He decrees a matter, then He simply says to it:*
*"Be," and it is.*

Qur'an 19:34-35

God was never to acquire a son. He was never to be debased with paternity in the human fashion as the result of a relationship with a woman. God is the Creator. When He creates something it's not as husband and wife create a son, but rather with His all-powerful word He simply says "Be!" and it happens.

*Jesus, Son of Mary,*
*was no more than a messenger of God...*
*God is only One God,*
*be He glorified that He should have a son!*

Qur'an 4:171

Once again the Unity of God and His eternal nature is stated. He would never add a son to Himself like the pagan gods had the habit of doing by having relations with goddesses and human females. He is sufficient in Himself. He would never stoop down to have relations with a woman. This is blasphemy. God is eternal and transcendent. He has never and will never acquire or add something to Himself or His Being.

Being called "Son of God" in the *Zaboor* meant that God was calling the person into a special relationship with Him to accomplish a certain mission or task. Salomon was called God's son in the following verse:

*I [God] will be his [Solomon's] father,*
*and he shall be my son.*
*If he commit iniquity,*
*I will chasten him with the rod of men,*
*and with the stripes of the children of men:*

2 Samuel 7:14 (KJV)

Here obviously God is not saying He had relations with Solomon's mother, Bathsheba, in order to be Solomon's father. Clearly it was King David who was Solomon's biological father. Rather, God was stating that He had a clear purpose for Solomon's life and therefore would treat Solomon as He'd treat His own son.

> *The Jews said: "Ezra is the son of God,"*
> *and the Nazarenes said "The Messiah is the son of God..."*
> *They have taken their Priests and Monks*
> *to be patrons besides God,*
> *and the Messiah, Son of Mary,*
> *while they were only commanded to serve One god,*
> *there is no god except He...*

Qur'an 9:30-31

This verse is in the context of Christians worshipping and adoring saints and human religions leaders, a practice common in the apostate Christian Church of the Dark Ages in Europe when the Qur'an was being revealed. The Qur'an logically protests against this blasphemous practice. At the same time, the Qur'an was written against the backdrop of Arabian paganism where there were male and female gods copulating and having god children. This is what the Qur'an is speaking out against. Needless to say, the concept of God having a son by cohabitation with a woman is just as abhorrent to Christians as to Muslims.

By trying to explain an act that only God can explain, we "play" God. Just because our finite minds are incapable of understanding the enormity of God we desperately limit God and try to "explain" acts that we in all honesty can't understand. This leads us into some turbulent waters of disagreement! Our humanity encroaches upon us and instead of just saying that we are incapable of explaining, we spin some tall argument in favor or against a specific doctrine! This leads to a vicious cycle of hopelessness! For only God, can create something out of nothing!

The Qur'an stance against calling anyone "Son of God" is to protest the blasphemy of saying that God would procreate in the human sense. Christians also are obviously horrified by that thought. So what do the Gospels mean when they use the term "Son of God"? How is it used? Who uses it? And to whom are they referring?

In the Gospels, Jesus only rarely refers to himself as "the son" and never as "Son of God." In fact, it was mostly Satan (Matthew 4:3,6; Luke 4:3,9), the demons (Matthew 8:29; Mark 3:11; Luke 4:41) and his enemies who mocked him with the title "Son of God" (Matthew 26:63 &

27:40,43,54; Mark 15:39; Luke 22:70; John 19:7). There are also a few examples of believers who called Jesus "Son of God":

## The angel Gabriel
*"The Holy Spirit will come upon you,*
*and the power of the Most High will overshadow you.*
*So the holy one to be born will be called the Son of God.*

Luke 1:35 (NIV)

The Gospel uses the exact same wording as in the Creation story in Genesis (as mentioned in the chapter "Son of Mary") and relates the idea of Jesus being called Son of God to the miracle of his virgin birth by comparing it to the creation of the first man, Adam, who is also called "Son of God" later in this same Gospel (Luke 3:38). Here "Son of God" means being directly created by God rather than being conceived in the normal human fashion.

## John the disciple
*But these are written that you may believe*
*that Jesus is the Messiah, the Son of God,*
*and that by believing you may have life in his name.*

John 20:31 (NIV)

John the disciple (as opposed to John the Baptist) was very close to Jesus during his years of healing, casting out demons, teaching, and resurrecting the dead. He had first hand experience to confirm that Jesus was in fact sent by God with a message for mankind and that he was especially anointed by God.

In other words, John wrote about Jesus so that those who read the Gospel would believe that he was the Messiah which he equates with "Son of God" which both mean anointed and set apart by God for a special mission. He most certainly doesn't mean in this passage that Jesus was biologically the Son of God in any way. Rather, John wants us to believe in the spiritual mission of the Messiah, or Son of God, as demonstrated in his life and works.

## The apostle Paul
*He was powerfully demonstrated*
*to be Son of God spiritually, set apart*
*by his having been resurrected from the dead;*

*he is Yeshua [Jesus] the Messiah, our Lord.*

Romans 1:4 (CJB)

Paul states that the ultimate mission of the Messiah and reason why he was called "Son of God" was a spiritual one based on the fact that God used him as an example of His power to resurrect the dead and take them to heaven, that death is not the end for the believer. This verse also clearly has nothing to do with procreation or biological sonship.

### The Disciples after Jesus calmed a storm
*Then they that were in the ship*
*came and worshipped him, saying,*
*Of a truth thou art the Son of God.*

Matthew 14:33 (KJV)

Here, once again, the disciples are recognizing that Jesus was special by the miracles God allowed him to do: in this case walking on water and calming a storm. It was these acts rather than anything to do with Jesus' parentage that caused the disciples to call him the Son of God. Again emphasizing that for them the phrase had nothing to do with the blasphemous concept of God engendering offspring.

### Nathanael the disciple
*...Rabbi, thou art the Son of God;*
*thou art the King of Israel.*

John 1:49 (KJV)

Here the disciple, Nathanael, reacts to his first encounter with Jesus and the fact that Jesus was able to probe his heart and mind. Nathanael associates "Son of God" with "King of Israel" another messianic appellation similar to "Son of David" with all the special things associated with the work of the Messiah.

### Martha, sister of Jesus' friend Lazarus
*"Yes, Lord," she replied,*
*"I believe that you are the Messiah, the Son of God,*
*who is to come into the world."*

John 11:27 (NIV)

As with the previous examples, Martha places "Messiah" and "Son of God" together thus associating their meanings thus clarifying once again that for the contemporaries of Jesus, "Son of God" was messianic and not biological.

### Mark
*The beginning of the good news about*
*Jesus the Messiah, the Son of God.*

Mark 1:1 (NIV)

Mark makes it clear from the beginning of the Gospel that whenever one sees "Son of God" one should understand "Messiah", the anointed one specially sent by God to accomplish an important task.

### Simon Peter the disciple
*When Jesus came to the region of Caesarea Philippi,*
*he asked his disciples,*
*"Who do people say the Son of Man is?"*
*They replied, "Some say John the Baptist;*
*others say Elijah; and still others,*
*Jeremiah or one of the prophets."*
*"But what about you?" he asked. "Who do you say I am?"*
*Simon Peter answered, "You are the Messiah,*
*the son of the living God."*
*Jesus replied, "Blessed are you, Simon son of Jonah,*
*for this was not revealed to you by flesh and blood,...*
*Then he ordered his disciples not to tell anyone*
*that he was the Messiah.*

Matthew 16:13-17,20 (NIV)

Jesus starts off by calling himself the "Son of Man". In fact, this is Jesus' favorite title for himself as he calls himself "Son of Man" 81 times in the gospels. In answer to Jesus' question, the disciples give a list of what some others are calling him: John the Baptist, Elijah, Jeremiah, or one of the other prophets. When Peter then steps up and calls Jesus the Messiah, the Son of God, Jesus acknowledges that only God could've revealed this to Peter. Again this reinforces the fact that the Messiah was a spiritual title for a special prophet.

When Jesus then goes on to tell them that it's not time yet to reveal to others that he's the Messiah, he in essence is stating that while both "Messiah" and "Son of God" have the same meaning, "Messiah" is the preferred term of the two. However, Jesus goes on to demonstrate that he prefers neither "Messiah" nor "Son of God" but rather "Son of Man."

The final example of Jesus preferring the title "Son of Man" comes near the end of the Gospels when Jesus is before the Jewish counsel being accused of being a false messiah.

*...The high priest said to him,*
*"I charge you under oath by the living God:*
*Tell us if you are the Messiah, the Son of God."*
*"You have said so," Jesus replied. "But I say to all of you:*
*From now on you will see the Son of Man*
*sitting at the right hand of the Mighty One*
*and coming on the clouds of heaven."*

Matthew 26:63-64 (NIV)

Right at the end, while on trial for his life, his accusers again equate the terms "Messiah" and "Son of God." Jesus doesn't deny either as he is the Messiah/Son of God with all that means for the mission God has given him, but he then goes on to reinforce that the best title for him is "Son of Man."

In fact, Jesus is quoting from an apocalyptic reference when he calls himself the "Son of Man":

*I saw in the night visions,*
*and, behold, one like the Son of Man*
*came with the clouds of heaven,*
*and came to the Ancient of days,*
*and they brought him near before him.*

Daniel 7:13 (KJV)

Both Daniel and the Revelation of Jesus Christ are Biblical books of prophecies revealing what will happen at the end of the world. The Revelation of Jesus Christ also uses the term "Son of Man" in the same sense as Daniel:

*And I looked, and behold a white cloud,*
*and upon the cloud one sat like unto the Son of Man,*

*having on his head a golden crown, and in his hand a sharp sickle.*
*And another angel came out of the temple,*
*crying with a loud voice to him that sat on the cloud,*
*Thrust in thy sickle, and reap:*
*for the time is come for thee to reap;*
*for the harvest of the earth is ripe.*

Revelation of Jesus Christ 14:14-15 (KJV)

Clearly, Daniel 7:13, Matthew 26:64, and Revelation 14:14 are all speaking of the same event: the return of Jesus the Messiah to judge the world. However, instead of the synonymous terms "Son of David," "Son of God," or even "Messiah," the preferred term used by Jesus and the Prophets is "Son of Man."

## CONCLUSION

In conclusion, the Jesus of the Qur'an and the Gospels is not the Son of God in the sense of God begetting biologically or procreating in the human fashion. This is blasphemous to both Christians and Muslims. The Gospels do use the term "Son of God" to refer to Jesus in a figurative sense relating to his closeness to God. In fact, it is mostly Satan, evil spirits, and Jesus' enemies who call him "the Son of God". When Jesus' friends call him "Son of God" it is always in reference to his mission as the Messiah and certainly does not imply that God in any way had a son by cohabitation.

Finally, Jesus doesn't use the phrase "Son of God", but prefers to call himself "the Son of Man" which has a special relation to his role in the end times on the Day of Judgment.

# To Die or Not to Die

*And Jesus cried out again*
*with a loud voice*
*and yielded up his spirit.*

Matthew 27:50 (ESV)

*And their saying: "We have killed the Messiah,*
*Jesus, Son of Mary, messenger of God!"*
*And they had not killed him,*
*nor crucified him,...*

Qur'an 4:157

*For God said: "O Jesus,*
*I will terminate your life,*
*and raise you to Me..."*

Qur'an 3:55

The question of the death and crucifixion of Jesus the Messiah is one that appears to definitively divide Christians and Muslims. Most Muslims will say that Jesus was not killed or crucified, while Christians will say that he was. The Muslim belief is based upon one verse:

*And their saying: "We have killed the Messiah,*
*Jesus, Son of Mary, messenger of God!"*
*And they had not killed him,*
*nor crucified him,*
*but it appeared to them as if they had.*
*And those who dispute are in doubt regarding him,*

*they have no knowledge except to follow conjecture;*
*they did not kill him for a certainty.*

Qur'an 4:157.

On the other hand, Christians base their belief that Jesus was killed and crucified on four chapters in the Gospels (*Injeel*): Matthew 27, Mark 15, Luke 23 and John 19. Can this apparent contradiction be reconciled?

First of all, Qur'an 4:157 doesn't say that Jesus didn't die, that he wasn't killed, or that he wasn't crucified. What it does say is that "they" didn't do it. So who are they? In studying any difficult passage of scripture, the first thing one must do is examine the surrounding verses.

Qur'an 4:153 starts off by talking about the "people of the Book" (*ahl al Kitab*). This phrase is used in the Qur'an to refer to both Christians and Jews. In verses 153-156 it becomes clear that in this case "the people of the Book" or "they" or "them" or "their" is referring to the Jews. It talks about "Moses" and the "calf" and the "mount" and the "covenant" and the "Sabbath" and "saying about Mary a great falsehood." So when we finally come to verse 157 it is a continuation of the previous accounts of time when the Jews had wandered from the path of God.

In other words, Qur'an 4:157 is saying that the Jews didn't kill or crucify Jesus, but it seemed to them as if they had. There are various theories that have been put forth on the issue of "appeared to them as if they had" (*shubbiha lahum*), but I believe it is simple. The Jews in Medina in Muhammad's day were claiming that Jesus couldn't have been the Messiah because they had killed him. In fact, God is trying to clarify this misconception on the part of the Jews in Medina.

The Qur'an is simply stating that despite what was being said to try and prove Jesus wasn't the Messiah, the claim by the Jews that they had killed and crucified Jesus was false, even though it recognizes that there was a reason the Jews could have thought that. The Gospels back this up. When the Jews tried Jesus in their courts they found him guilty, but then they had to take him to the Roman governor, Pilate, because they didn't have the authority to apply the death penalty. As they say to Pilate in the Gospel:

*The Jews therefore said unto him,*
*It is not lawful for us*
*to put any man to death.*

John 18:31 (KJV)

In other words, the Jews found him guilty of death by their laws and wanted to kill him, but they couldn't. They needed to get the Romans to do it for them. The Gospels confirm what the Qur'an states that it was in fact the Romans who actually nailed Jesus the Messiah to the cross and not the Jews.

*Then the soldiers of the governor took Jesus...*
*And they stripped him, and put on him a scarlet robe.*
*And when they had platted a crown of thorns,*
*they put it upon his head...*
*And they spit upon him...*
*And after that they had mocked him,*
*they...led him away to crucify him.*

Matthew 27: 27-31 (KJV)

*And so Pilate, willing to content the people...*
*delivered Jesus, when he had scourged him,*
*to be crucified.*
*And the soldiers led him away...*
*to crucify him...*
*And it was the third hour,*
*and they crucified him.*

Mark 15:15-25 (KJV)

*But they were urgent,*
*demanding with loud cries*
*that he should be crucified.*
*And their voices prevailed.*
*So Pilate decided that their demand should be granted...*
*He delivered Jesus over to their will...*
*Two others, who were criminals,*
*were led away to be put to death with him.*
*And when they came to the place*
*that is called The Skull,*
*there they crucified him, and the criminals,*
*one on his right and one on his left...*
*The soldiers also mocked him...*

Luke 23:33-36 (ESV)

*Where they crucified him,*
*and two other with him,*
*on either side one,*
*and Jesus in the midst...*
*Then the soldiers, when they had crucified Jesus,*
*took his garments, and made four parts,*
*to every soldier a part...*
*These things therefore the soldiers did.*

John 19:18-24 (KJV)

But this isn't the whole story. While it's true that the Jews wanted to kill Jesus and the Romans actually crucified him, Jesus' death actually went much deeper, all the way back to a scheme or plan on the part of God. And in the end, it is only God who can take life or give it. The Qur'an confirms this with a powerful statement about God's plan to terminate Jesus' life.

*And they schemed and God schemed,*
*but God is the best schemer.*
*For God said: "O Jesus, I will terminate your life,*
*and raise you to Me,*
*and cleanse you of those who have rejected,*
*and make those who have followed you*
*above those who have rejected*
*until the Day of Resurrection.*
*Then to Me is your return, all of you,*
*so I will judge between you*
*in what it was that you disputed."*

Qur'an 3:54-55

People scheme and make their own plans, but ultimately God is the best schemer, plotter and planner. According to these verses, it was the plan of God that Jesus not only die, but that he be raised up to God and cleansed or purified. Then, at the Day of Resurrection, all things that have been disputed—including whether the Messiah really did die or not—will be judged by God.

Most English translations misinterpret the Arabic word "*Mutawaffeeka*" as "I will recall you" or "I will take thee" or "I am gathering thee" or "I am going to terminate the period of your stay (on earth)". However, the literal meaning is "I will cause you to die" or "I will terminate your life." The Arabic root is "*Waw-Fa-Ya*" which creates the verb "*tawaffa*" which means "to die."

The same mistranslation also happens in most English versions of Qur'an 5:117 where Jesus the Son of Mary says:

*"I only said to them*
*what You commanded me to say,*
*that you shall serve God my Lord and your Lord;*
*and I was witness over them*
*as long as I was with them,*
*but when You terminated my life,*
*You were watcher over them.*
*You are witness over all things."*

The phrase "You terminated my life" is the Arabic word "*tawaffaytanee*" from the same Arabic root "*Waw-Fa-Ya*" and the same verb "*tawaffa*" as in Qur'an 3:55.

This means that not only is Qur'an 4:157 clearing up the misconception that the Jews killed and crucified the Messiah when it was really the Romans, but these two verses go on to clarify that Jesus' death was part of God's plan because it was God who "schemed" and terminated the earthly life of the Son of Mary.

The Gospels state that it was only because of God's ultimate authority that Jesus himself lays down his own life. He goes willingly to his death because it was God's plan.

*"... I [Jesus] lay down my life that I may take it up again.*
*No one takes it from me,*
*but I lay it down of my own accord.*
*I have authority to lay it down,*
*and I have authority to take it up again.*
*This charge I have received from my Father."*

John 10:17-18 (ESV)

And again, when Pilate is speaking to Jesus just before handing him over to the soldiers to be crucified, the Messiah restates that it is only because of God's sovereignty that the Romans can crucify him:

*So Pilate said to him, "You will not speak to me?*
*Do you not know that I have authority to release you*
*and authority to crucify you?"*

*Jesus answered him,*
*"You would have no authority over me at all*
*unless it had been given you from above..."*

John 19:10-11 (ESV)

All four Gospels record that when Jesus died on the cross it was him yielding up his spirit, no one took it from him:

*And Jesus cried out again with a loud voice*
*and yielded up his spirit.*

Matthew 27:50 (ESV)

*And Jesus uttered a loud cry*
*and breathed his last.*

Mark 15:37 (ESV)

*Then Jesus,*
*calling out with a loud voice,*
*said, "Father, into your hands*
*I commit my spirit!"*
*and having said this*
*he breathed his last.*

Luke 23:46 (ESV)

*...Jesus...said, "It is finished,"*
*and he bowed his head*
*and gave up his spirit...*
*But when they came to Jesus*
*and saw that he was already dead,*
*they did not break his legs.*
*But one of the soldiers*
*pierced his side with a spear,*
*and at once there came out*
*blood and water.*

John 19:30-34 (ESV)

## <u>CONCLUSION</u>

In conclusion, the Jesus of the Qur'an and the Gospels wasn't killed or crucified by the Jews. It only seemed to them that they did because they wanted to, but didn't have the authority. In fact it was the Romans who committed the act, unwittingly fulfilling God's plan for the Messiah to die and give up his spirit back to God.

# Resurrector

*And Jesus said unto her,*
*"I am the resurrection, and the life:*
*he that believeth in me*
*though he were dead, yet shall he live."*

John 11:25 (KJV)

*"And peace be upon me the day I was born,*
*and the day I die, and the day I am resurrected alive."*
*Such was Jesus, Son of Mary,*
*and this is the truth of the matter in which they doubt.*

Qur'an 19:33-34

The Qur'an mentions in two places that the Messiah, Jesus, Son of Mary, was given power to resurrect the dead by the permission of God:

*...and I [Jesus] heal the blind and the lepers,*
*and give life to the dead*
*with the permission of God,...*

Qur'an 3:49

*"...and you [Jesus] would heal the blind and the leper*
*with My permission;*
*and you would bring out the dead*
*with My permission...*

Qur'an 5:110

The Gospels recount three examples of the Messiah raising the dead.

*And it came to pass the day after,*
*that he went into a city called Nain;*
*and many of his disciples went with him, and much people.*
*Now when he came nigh to the gate of the city,*
*behold, there was a dead man carried out,*
*the only son of his mother, and she was a widow:*
*and much people of the city was with her.*

*And when the Lord saw her,*
*he had compassion on her,*
*and said unto her, Weep not.*
*And he came and touched the bier:*
*and they that bare him stood still.*
*And he said, Young man, I say unto thee, Arise*

*And he that was dead sat up, and began to speak.*
*And he delivered him to his mother.*
*And there came a fear on all:*
*and they glorified God, saying,*
*That a great prophet is risen up among us;*
*and, That God hath visited his people.*

Luke 7:11-16 (KJV)

Jesus comes unexpectedly upon a funeral procession where the mother of the dead boy had already lost her husband and now lost the only son she had. By losing both husband and only son she would have no means of support and be destined to a life of poverty. Jesus recognizes this all immediately through the power of God and being moved with compassion raises the dead boy to life.

*And, behold, there cometh one of the rulers of the synagogue,*
*Jairus by name; and when he saw him, he fell at his feet,*
*And besought him greatly, saying,*
*My little daughter lieth at the point of death:*
*I pray thee, come and lay thy hands on her,*
*that she may be healed; and she shall live.*
*And Jesus went with him;*
*and much people followed him, and thronged him...*

*...there came from the ruler of the synagogue's house*
*certain which said, Thy daughter is dead:*
*why troublest thou the Master any further?*
*As soon as Jesus heard the word that was spoken,*
*he saith unto the ruler of the synagogue,*
*Be not afraid, only believe.*
*And he suffered no man to follow him,*
*save Peter, and James, and John the brother of James.*
*And he cometh to the house of the ruler of the synagogue,*
*and seeth the tumult, and them that wept and wailed greatly.*
*And when he was come in, he saith unto them,*
*Why make ye this ado, and weep?*
*the damsel is not dead, but sleepeth.*
*And they laughed him to scorn.*
*But when he had put them all out,*
*he taketh the father and the mother of the damsel,*
*and them that were with him,*
*and entereth in where the damsel was lying.*
*And he took the damsel by the hand,*
*and said unto her, Talitha cumi;*
*which is, being interpreted,*
*Damsel, I say unto thee, arise.*
*And straightway the damsel arose, and walked;*
*for she was of the age of twelve years.*
*And they were astonished with a great astonishment.*
*And he charged them straitly that no man should know it;*
*and commanded that something should be given her to eat.*

Mark 5:22-42 (KJV)

To Jesus, death is nothing but a sleep, a peaceful place of rest. There is no need to weep and cry as death is simply God putting some of his children to sleep for the night knowing He will wake them in the morning. Jesus demonstrates that for anyone having the Spirit of God in them, raising the dead is as simple as waking someone from sleep as the power of God who created all things by a single word can just as easily bring someone to life again.

The last story in the Gospels of Jesus resurrecting someone is given in detail in John 11. Lazarus, one of Jesus' friends, was sick and died. Four days later, after Lazarus was already in the tomb, Jesus and his disciples show up where Lazarus' two grieving sisters take them out to the grave. The oldest sister, Martha, questions why Jesus didn't come heal his friend

Lazarus. She had heard the stories of Jesus healing people and knew that God had given him this power, so she wonders why he didn't take the time to come heal one of his closest friends, her brother Lazarus.

*Jesus saith unto her, Thy brother shall rise again.*
*Martha saith unto him, I know that he shall rise again*
*in the resurrection at the last day.*
*Jesus said unto her, I am the resurrection, and the life:*
*he that believeth in me, though he were dead, yet shall he live:*
*And whosoever liveth and believeth in me shall never die.*
*Believest thou this?*
*She saith unto him, Yea, Lord:*
*I believe that thou art the Christ, the Son of God,*
*which should come into the world...*

*Jesus therefore again groaning in himself cometh to the grave.*
*It was a cave, and a stone lay upon it.*
*Jesus said, Take ye away the stone.*
*Martha, the sister of him that was dead,*
*saith unto him, Lord, by this time he stinketh:*
*for he hath been dead four days.*
*Jesus saith unto her, Said I not unto thee,*
*that, if thou wouldest believe,*
*thou shouldest see the glory of God?*
*Then they took away the stone*
*from the place where the dead was laid.*

*And Jesus lifted up his eyes, and said,*
*Father, I thank thee that thou hast heard me.*
*And I knew that thou hearest me always:*
*but because of the people which stand by I said it,*
*that they may believe that thou hast sent me.*
*And when he thus had spoken,*
*he cried with a loud voice, Lazarus, come forth.*
*And he that was dead came forth,*
*bound hand and foot with grave clothes:*
*and his face was bound about with a napkin.*
*Jesus saith unto them, Loose him, and let him go.*

John 11:23-27, 38-44 (KJV)

Jesus states here that he knows that it is through prayer connecting him with God that he was given the ability to raise the dead to life again. And Jesus prays out loud so that everyone else will recognize that this resurrection power comes from God. The Qur'an states numerous times that only God can give life to the dead:

*The One who has created me, He will guide me.*
*And He is the One who feeds me and gives me to drink.*
*And if I am sick, He is the One who cures me.*
*And the One who will make me die and then bring me to life.*

Qur'an 26:78-81

*Say: "My Lord casts with the truth.*
*He is the Knower of all secrets."*
*Say: "The truth has come;*
*while falsehood can neither*
*initiate anything, nor resurrect."*

Qur'an 34:48-49

*It is indeed Us who resurrect the dead...*

Qur'an 36:12

*"...Who can resurrect the bones while they are dust?"*
*Say: "The One who has made them*
*in the first place will resurrect them.*
*He is fully aware of every creation."*

Qur'an 36:78-79

*...But God is the ally,*
*and He is the One who resurrects the dead,*
*and He is able to do all things.*
*And anything you dispute in then*
*its judgment shall be with God.*
*Such is God my Lord.*
*In Him I place my trust,*
*and to Him I repent.*

Qur'an 42:9-10

The power to resurrect is an exceptional gift God has given to Jesus. Only God has the power to give life to the dead, but he has shared that with Jesus making him someone special indeed.

But what about Jesus' own death? We found out in the last chapter, that he really did die as a part of God's plan. In fact, he was condemned to death by the Jews, but since they didn't have the authority they convinced the Romans to crucify Jesus for them. But did he stay dead, or did did God raise him back to life?

*"And peace be upon me the day I was born,*
*and the day I die, and the day I am resurrected alive."*
*Such was Jesus, Son of Mary,*
*and this is the truth of the matter in which they doubt.*

Qur'an 19:33-34

Jesus himself states that he will die and be resurrected and that it will become a matter of faith and doubt. But when will he be resurrected? Has it already happened, or will it be at the end of the world when everyone else is raised? The two parallel passages that follow first discuss the Messiah's death and then state afterwards that God will raise Jesus to Himself.

*For God said: "O Jesus, I will terminate your life,*
*and raise you to Me,*
*and cleanse you of those who have rejected,*
*and make those who have followed you*
*above those who have rejected*
*until the Day of Resurrection.*
*Then to Me is your return, all of you,*
*so I will judge between you*
*in what it was that you disputed."*

Qur'an 3:55

*And their saying: "We have killed the Messiah,*
*Jesus, Son of Mary, messenger of God!"*
*And they had not killed him, nor crucified him,*
*but it appeared to them as if they had.*
*And those who dispute are in doubt regarding him,*
*they have no knowledge except to follow conjecture;*

*they did not kill him for a certainty.*
*Instead, God had raised him to Himself;*
*and God is Noble, Wise.*
*And from the people of the Book*
*are those who refused to believe*
*in him before his death,*
*and on the Day of Resurrection*
*he will be witness against them.*

Qur'an 4:157-159

The verb "raise you to me" and "raised him to Himself" is the same in both passages: *rafa'a* from the Arabic root *Ra-Fa-Ayn*. The meaning of *rafa'a* is: to raise/uplift/elevate, to take up, to lift/hoist, extol, uprear it, rear it, make it high/lofty, take it and carry it, raise into view, to exalt, to advance, bring a thing near presenting or offering, to bring forward, to take away, disappear, trace back, honor, show regard to, to introduce, refine, to make known, go upwards (from *myQuran* for the iPad).

Both passages also recognize that this subject—the death and resurrection of the Messiah—will be a subject of dispute, doubt, conjecture and cause of disbelief. While the topic is complicated, with a careful examination of the texts we can once again come to a common understanding between the Qur'an and the Gospels.

In Qur'an 3:55 it is clear that the raising up (*rafa'a*) occurs after God terminates Jesus' life (*mutawaffeeka*). Therefore, logically, it also involves a resurrection since it is unlikely that God would raise a corpse to Himself. And we've seen that with God, creating life or resurrecting are easy: He simply says "Be" and it is (*kun faya kun*).

So since the Scriptures, as the Words of God, have to be consistent with themselves, the *rafa'a* in Qur'an 4:158 (which is past tense) also had to have been after Jesus' death. While it says the Jews didn't kill or crucify the Messiah, Jesus did die. This *rafa'a* also must involve Jesus' resurrection from the dead before being taken up to God which is a part of God's plan.

Qur'an 4:159 also states that some of the "people of the Book" (Jews and Christians) "refused to believe in him [Jesus] before his [Jesus'] death" before the Day of Resurrection when all the other dead will be raised. Then, all will be judged by God according to what they have done with Jesus himself as a witness against them.

So, while it is complicated to understand—and the Qur'an recognizes that it will cause disputes—we can look at the different verses in the Qur'an that speak on the subject and recognize that Jesus did die and was resurrected by God before being raised to His presence. Thus, once again, there is harmony between the different Holy Books. The Gospels record the resurrection of Jesus in detail (Matthew 28, Mark 16, Luke 24 and John 20).

> *Now upon the first day of the week,*
> *very early in the morning,*
> *they came unto the sepulchre,*
> *bringing the spices which they had prepared,*
> *and certain others with them.*
> *And they found the stone rolled away from the sepulchre.*
> *And they entered in, and found not the body of the Lord Jesus.*
> *And it came to pass, as they were much perplexed thereabout,*
> *behold, two men stood by them in shining garments:*
> *And as they were afraid, and bowed down their faces to the earth,*
> *they said unto them, Why seek ye the living among the dead?*
> *He is not here, but is risen:*
> *remember how he spake unto you when he was yet in Galilee,*
> *Saying, The Son of Man must be delivered*
> *into the hands of sinful men, and be crucified,*
> *and the third day rise again.*

Luke 24:1-7 (KJV)

Jesus was crucified and died on a Friday and laid in a tomb (sepulchre). But on Sunday, he was resurrected through the power of God who opened the tomb by rolling away the stone. Jesus had warned the disciples ahead of time, using his favorite title for himself, Son of Man. After hearing the message from the angels, the others left.

> *But Mary stood without at the sepulchre weeping:*
> *and as she wept, she stooped down,*
> *and looked into the sepulchre,*
> *And seeth two angels in white sitting,*
> *the one at the head, and the other at the feet,*
> *where the body of Jesus had lain.*
> *And they say unto her, Woman, why weepest thou?*
> *She saith unto them, Because they have taken away my LORD,*
> *and I know not where they have laid him.*
> *And when she had thus said, she turned herself back,*
> *and saw Jesus standing, and knew not that it was Jesus.*
> *Jesus saith unto her, Woman,*
> *why weepest thou? whom seekest thou?*

*She, supposing him to be the gardener, saith unto him,*
*Sir, if thou have borne him hence,*
*tell me where thou hast laid him, and I will take him away.*
*Jesus saith unto her, Mary.*
*She turned herself, and saith unto him,*
*Rabboni; which is to say, Master.*
*Jesus saith unto her, Touch me not;*
*or I am not yet ascended to my Father:*
*but go to my brethren, and say unto them,*
*I ascend unto my Father, and your Father;*
*and to my God, and your God.*

John 20:11-17 (KJV)

Jesus takes the time to reassure one of his most faithful disciples, Mary, and to comfort her. Jesus also reaffirms that the God of the disciples is also Jesus' God. After several more meetings with the disciples, Jesus is finally taken up to heaven.

*And when he [Jesus] had spoken these things,*
*while they beheld, he was taken up;*
*and a cloud received him out of their sight.*
*And while they looked steadfastly toward heaven as he went up,*
*behold, two men stood by them in white apparel;*
*Which also said, Ye men of Galilee,*
*why stand ye gazing up into heaven?*
*this same Jesus, which is taken up from you into heaven,*
*shall so come in like manner as ye have seen him go into heaven.*

Acts 1:9-11 (KJV)

### CONCLUSION

In conclusion, the Jesus of the Qur'an and the Gospels had the ability to raise the dead through the power of God since only the Creator can resurrect. This made Jesus unusually special indeed. And as part of God's plan, after causing Jesus to die, God raised Jesus to life again and took him up to Heaven where he will stay until he comes back on the Day of Resurrection. This is completely and irrevocably supported by both the Qur'an and the Gospels.

# Word of God

*In the beginning was the Word,*
*and the Word was with God,*
*and the Word was God...*
*And the Word was made flesh,*
*and dwelt among us...*

John 1:1,14 (KJV)

*...Jesus, Son of Mary,*
*was no more than a messenger of God*
*and the fulfillment of His word to Mary*
*and a Spirit from Him...*

Qur'an 4:171

Jesus is called a word from God or His word directly three times in the Qur'an (3:39, 3:45, 4:171). The Arabic is *kalima* and is used in the plural many times in the Qur'an to speak of messages, usually ones sent by God, or oaths taken by people. It is only used to refer to one person: Jesus, Son of Mary.

There is also one verse in the Qur'an that might be speaking of Jesus as the word:

*Such was Jesus, Son of Mary:*
*a statement of truth*
*concerning which they doubt.*

Qur'an 19:34 (Pickthall)

This verse is interesting because with a small change of vowel pointing the phrase in the original Arabic "statement of truth" (*qawla'l-*

*haqqi*) becomes "word of truth (*qawlu'l-haqqi*). Of course, the original Qur'an didn't have vowel pointing so either meaning is possible. If it really is *qawlu'l-haqqi* then Jesus is the word of truth which has been a source of dispute through the centuries.

The verse following 19:34 gives evidence that the phrase should be "word of truth", especially when compared with Qur'an 3:45-47.

> *God was never to take a son, be He glorified.*
> *If He decrees a matter,*
> *then He simply says to it:*
> *'Be,' and it is.*

Qur'an 19:35

> *And the angels said: "O Mary,*
> *God gives you glad tidings of a word from Him.*
> *His name is the Messiah, Jesus, Son of Mary.*
> *Honorable in this world and in the Hereafter,*
> *and from among those who are made close..."*
> *He said: "It is thus that God creates*
> *what He wills,*
> *when He decrees a command,*
> *He merely says to it*
> *'Be,' and it is."*

Qur'an 3:45,47

Both are talking about Jesus as a word or statement (word?) and both end with the same phrase: "Be, and it is" (*kun faya kun*). This is God's creative word that is always involved in Him creating something from nothing:

*Kun faya kun* is used four other times in the Qur'an and all refer to God's creative power where he commands or says to something simply "Be, and it is."

> *Initiator of the heavens and the earth,*
> *when He decrees a command,*
> *He merely says to it:*
> *'Be,' and it is.*

Qur'an 2:117

*Indeed , Our saying to a thing,*
*If We wanted it, is that We say to it:*
*'Be,' and it is.*

Qur'an 16:40

*His command, when He wants anything,*
*is to say to it: 'Be,' and it is.*

Qur'an 36:82

*He is the One who gives life and death.*
*And when He decides upon anything,*
*He simply says to it:*
*'Be,' and it is.*

Qur'an 40:68

So the Qur'an associates the word (*kalima*) with the creative force of God where He simply speaks and creation happens (*kun faya kun*).

It's interesting that the Gospels only refer to the Word of God in a single chapter. In the opening verses of the Gospel of John, the Word is uncreated, existing from the beginning with God and is the means God uses to create. Both also state that John the Baptist (*Yaya*) will come announcing or authenticating the word of God.

*In the beginning was the Word,*
*and the Word was with God,*
*and the Word was God.*
*The same was in the beginning with God.*
*All things were made by him;*
*and without him was not any thing made that was made.*
*In him was life; and the life was the light of men.*
*And the light shineth in darkness;*
*and the darkness comprehended it not.*
*There was a man sent from God,*
*whose name was John.*
*The same came for a witness,*
*to bear witness of the Light,*
*that all men through him might believe.*

John 1:1-7 (KJV)

*"God gives you glad tidings of John,
authenticating the word from God..."*

Qur'an 3:39

John was sent to witness to the Word from God, the creative power of God that was the source of life and light. The word of God is eternal, existing before creation because it was this word that God used to create the world out of nothing (*kun faya kun*).

But then, in order for humans to see God's creative power, God created another miracle, a human baby with no father, born of a virgin. And God placed His creative power in this human which is why Jesus could heal the sick and raise the dead by God's permission. It was the word of God in the miraculously created human body of Jesus that allowed Jesus to perform these miracles.

*And the Word was made flesh,
and dwelt among us...
full of grace and truth.
John bare witness of him, and cried, saying,
This was he of whom I spake,
He that cometh after me is preferred before me:
for he was before me.
And of his fulness have all we received,
and grace for grace.
For the law was given by Moses,
but grace and truth came by Jesus Christ.*

John 1:14-17 (KJV)

## <u>CONCLUSION</u>

In conclusion, the Jesus of the Qur'an and the Gospels is the word of God, meaning that God's creative power (*kun faya kun*) resides in his human body. John the Baptist (*Yaya*) witnessed to this fact that Jesus the Messiah was the creative word of God made flesh through a miraculous conception in the virgin Mary so that all peoples could get a glimpse of the creative power of God in action through the miracles of healing and raising the dead performed by the Messiah.

# Spirit of God

*But God hath revealed them unto us by his Spirit:*
*for the Spirit searcheth all things,*
*yea, the deep things of God.*

1 Corinthians 2:10 (KJV)

*Jesus, Son of Mary,*
*was no more than a messenger of God*
*and the fulfillment of His word to Mary*
*and a Spirit from Him.*

Qur'an 4:171

What is the Spirit of God (*Ruh Al-Lah*)? First of all, we know from both the Gospels and the Qur'an that the Spirit of God was involved in the creation, specifically of the first human being, Adam.

*The One who perfected everything He created*
*and he began the creation of man from clay...*
*and blew into him from His Spirit...*

Qur'an 32:7-9
(see also 15:28-29 and 38:71-72)

*In the beginning God created*
*the heaven and the earth.*
*And the earth was without form, and void;*
*and darkness was upon the face of the deep.*
*And the Spirit of God moved upon the face of the waters...*
*And the Lord God formed*

*man of the dust of the ground,*
*and breathed into his nostrils the breath of life;*
*and man became a living soul.*

Genesis 1:1-2:7 (KJV)

The two Hebrew words used here for Spirit and breath—*Ruah* and *nashamah*—both mean "wind" or "air." So God's essence, His breath, His life was placed into this being created from earth and the being, Adam, came to life.

In the creation of Adam, God forms him from the clay. He fashions the lifeless clay intimately and uniquely. He bestows on the lifeless form His image, and then He breaths into the clay His Spirit (*Ruah*). When God decides to form Jesus in the womb of a virgin, the same process takes place. However, instead of the clay, the body of the virgin becomes the housing complex into which God's Spirit (*Ruah Elohim*) enters. Thus the Spirit of God takes a definite and distinctive role in the formation of Adam and Jesus.

*...so We sent Our Spirit to her [Mary],*
*and he took on the shape of a human being in all similarity...*
*He said: "I am the messenger of your Lord,*
*to grant you the gift of a pure son."*

Qur'an 19:17-19

*And Mary said to the angel, "How will this be,*
*since I am a virgin?"*
*And the angel answered her, "The Holy Spirit will come upon you,*
*and the power of the Most High will overshadow you;*
*Therefore the child to be born will be called holy...*
*For nothing is impossible with God."*

Luke 1:34-35, 37 (NIV)

*And Mary, daughter of Imran,*
*who maintained the chastity of her private part,*
*so We blew into it from Our Spirit,*
*and she believed in the words of her Lord and His Books;*
*and she was of those who where dutiful.*

Qur'an 66:12

It's interesting that here we see first that the Spirit of God came to Mary in the shape of a human so we know that God's Spirit can appear in human form. Then that same Spirit, the Holy Spirit, comes upon Mary, overshadows her, and is blown into her womb to create Jesus. So Jesus was a combination of a direct creation of a physical man by God's power and the indwelling of His Spirit.

So what does that mean, to have the Spirit of God inside a person? In three places in the Qur'an it says about Jesus that God "supported him with the Holy Spirit" (Qur'an 2:87, 2:253 and 5:110). So the Spirit of God was Jesus' support: psychological, emotional, social, spiritual and physical. The Spirit gave Jesus the ability to think, feel, relate, pray and act just like God would if He could be contained in a three dimensional body.

> *But God hath revealed them unto us by his Spirit:*
> *for the Spirit searcheth all things,*
> *yea, the deep things of God.*
> *For what man knoweth the things of a man,*
> *save the spirit of man which is in him?*
> *Even so the things of God knoweth no man,*
> *but the Spirit of God.*
> *Now we have received, not the spirit of the world,*
> *but the spirit which is of God;*
> *that we might know the things*
> *that are freely given to us of God.*

1 Corinthians 2:10-12 (KJV)

The Qur'an talks about the attributes of God's Spirit: truth, strength, guidance, good news, authority, and knowledge.

> *Say: "The Holy Spirit has brought it down*
> *from your Lord with the truth,*
> *so that those who believe will be strengthened,*
> *and as a guidance and good news*
> *for those who have submitted.*

Qur'an 16:102

> *And they ask you concerning the Spirit.*
> *Say: "The Spirit is from the authority of my Lord;*
> *and the knowledge you were given was but very little."*

Qur'an 17:85

Both the Qur'an and the Gospels also say that Jesus is not only a messenger and a Word from God, but "a Spirit from Him" (Qur'an 4:171).

*Now the Lord [Jesus] is that Spirit:*
*and where the Spirit of the Lord is, there is liberty.*

2 Corinthians 3:17 (KJV)

Jesus IS the Spirit of God. Jesus is God's character, personality, essence, knowledge and power come down into a created form made in the womb of a virgin by God's mighty word "Be!"

*O people of the Book,*
*do not overstep in your system,*
*nor say about God except the truth.*
*Jesus, Son of Mary,*
*was no more than a messenger of God*
*and the fulfillment of His word to Mary*
*and a Spirit from Him.*
*So believe in God and His messengers,*
*and do not say: "Trinity."*
*Cease, for it is better for you.*
*God is only One god,*
*be He glorified that He should have a son!*
*To Him is all that is in the heavens and the earth;*
*and God is enough as a Caretaker.*

Qur'an 4:171

The word "trinity" here in the English translation is really the word "three" (*talata*) in the original Arabic. Interestingly, the word "trinity" doesn't appear either in the Bible or the Qur'an. It started being used by Christians about 400 years after Jesus. As this verse in the Qur'an clearly states, while there are three mysteries that are eternal—God (*Al-Lah*), the Word of God (*Kalimat Al-Lah*), and the Spirit of God (*Ruh Al-Lah*)—these are not three gods but rather expressions of a mystery inherent in the greatness of God Himself who is One. The Bible also talks of these three mysteries:

*In the beginning was the Word,*

*and the Word was with God,*
*and the Word was God...*
*And the Word was made flesh,*
*and dwelt among us...*

John 1:1,14 (KJV)

*Howbeit when he, the Spirit of truth,*
*is come, he will guide you into all truth:*
*for he shall not speak of himself;*
*but whatsoever he shall hear,*
*that shall he speak:*
*and he will shew you things to come.*

John 16:13 (KJV)

*And Jesus answered him,*
*The first of all the commandments is,*
*Hear, O Israel; The Lord our God is one Lord:*

Mark 12:29 (KJV)

Unfortunately, the doctrine of the Trinity has confused things for many Christians so that even though most will say they believe in one God, deep down they still think of God, God's Spirit and God's Word as three different beings rather than expressions of the Oneness of God. This allows them to think for example that Jesus is merciful and forgiving while God is harsh, severe and arbitrary. That's why many Christians pray to Jesus instead of to God, hoping that Jesus will put in a good word for them with God. This is a distortion of the character of God.

Rather Jesus came to show what God's character was like. By having God's Word dwell in his human body, Jesus was able to demonstrate God's power to heal and raise the dead through God's creative word "Be!" By having God's Spirit dwell in his human body, Jesus was able to demonstrate God's compassion, purity, mercy, grace, forgiveness and love.

When Jesus was talking with his disciples for the last time, they asked him the way to God (the "Father" in their terminology, signifying God as the Origin and Creator of all things) and to show them God.

*Thomas saith unto him,*
*Lord, we know not whither thou goest;*
*and how can we know the way?*

*Jesus saith unto him,*
*I am the way, the truth, and the life:*
*no man cometh unto the Father, but by me.*
*If ye had known me,*
*ye should have known my Father also:*
*and from henceforth ye know him,*
*and have seen him.*

*Philip saith unto him,*
*Lord, show us the Father, and it sufficeth us.*

*Jesus saith unto him,*
*Have I been so long time with you,*
*and yet hast thou not known me, Philip?*
*He that hath seen me hath seen the Father;*
*and how sayest thou then,*
*Show us the Father?*
*Believest thou not that I am in the Father,*
*and the Father in me?*
*The words that I speak unto you I speak not of myself:*
*but the Father that dwelleth in me,*
*he doeth the works.*

John 14:5-10 (KJV)

Clearly, Jesus knew that it was only because God's Word was in him that he spoke the message of God, it wasn't himself speaking. Jesus also knew that it was the indwelling of God's Spirit that allowed him to do the works he did. Jesus was not another God, but rather a vehicle for God to display His words and works to the world by the exact representation of His Spirit and Word in a human body created miraculously and specifically for this purpose.

*Let this mind be in you,*
*which was also in Christ Jesus:*
*Who, being in the form of God,*
*thought it not robbery to be equal with God:*
*But made himself of no reputation,*
*and took upon him the form of a servant,*
*and was made in the likeness of men*

Philippians 2:5-7 (KJV)

Finally, the Qur'an warns us to make the truth about God as revealed in His Books and by His Spirit as of the utmost importance. This belief should take precedence over family and friends and we should not be afraid, even of death, in our pursuit of the truth that will lead us to Paradise:

*You will not find any people*
*who believe in God and the Last Day*
*leaning towards those who oppose*
*God and His messenger,*
*even if they were their parents,*
*or their children,*
*or their siblings,*
*or their kin.*
*For these, He decrees faith into their hearts,*
*and supports them with a Spirit from Him,*
*and He admits them into estates*
*with rivers flowing beneath them;*
*abiding therein.*
*God is pleased with them,*
*and they are pleased with Him.*
*These are the party of God.*
*Most assuredly, the party of God are the winners.*

Qur'an 58:22

## **CONCLUSION**

In conclusion, the Jesus of the Qur'an and the Gospels is the Spirit of God. This doesn't mean that Jesus is an ethereal being in the supernatural world, but rather that he possesses the personality of God in the flesh: truth, strength, guidance, good news, authority, and knowledge. By dwelling in Jesus, humans were able to see God's character in person and know God through Jesus' words and acts which came from God. This has created confusion for Christians in the doctrine of the Trinity. Neither the Bible nor the Qur'an mention the Trinity but rather talk about three mysterious entities that are eternal: God (*Al-Lah*), the Word of God (*Kalimat Al-Lah*), and the Spirit of God (*Ruh Al-Lah*). How these interact and work is part of the mystery of God's greatness and Oneness. Finally, we are told that this truth as revealed by God's Spirit should be more important than any family ties if we want to inherit Paradise.

# Sign

*And the one who protected her chastity,*
*so We blew into her from Our Spirit,*
*and We made her and her son*
*a sign for the worlds.*

Qur'an 21:91

*And We made the Son of Mary and his mother a sign...*

Qur'an 23:50

The word "sign" (*aya*) is used over a hundred times in the Qur'an. It usually symbolizes something or someone that God is using to give evidence to base one's belief on. God wants us to have faith, but He doesn't expect us to have an unreasonable faith. He is the one who has given humans the ability to reason and think, question and doubt, analyze and debate.

*...It is thus that God clarifies for you*
*the revelations that you may think.*

Qur'an 2:219

*...Are the blind and the seer the same?*
*Do you not think?*

Qur'an 6:50

*...So tell the stories,*
*perhaps they will think.*

Qur'an 7:176

*...It is such that We clarify the revelations*
*for a people who think.*

Qur'an 10:24

*...In that are signs*
*For a people who think.*

Qur'an 13:3

Therefore, while in the end we can't understand everything, God gives us enough signs, examples, parables, and evidence to base our faith on. The Gospels echo this.

*Now faith is the substance of things hoped for,*
*the evidence of things not seen.*

Hebrews 11:1 (KJV)

The Book of Hebrews in the *Injeel* actually starts off by confirming what the Qur'an states: that Jesus is a sign for all people. God used Jesus as a parable to represent His being and glory to humans by placing His Spirit in a created human body.

*In the past God spoke to our ancestors*
*through the prophets*
*at many times and in various ways*
*but in these last days*
*He has spoken to us by His son,*
*whom He appointed heir of all things,*
*and through whom also he made the universe*
*The son is the radiance of God's glory*
*and the exact representation of His being,*
*sustaining all things by his powerful word.*
*After he had provided purification for sins,*
*he sat down at the right hand of the Majesty in heaven.*

Hebrews 1:1-3 (NIV)

Jesus was thus to be an example to all people up to the Day of Judgment or the "Hour" as the Qur'an says:

*And when the Son of Mary*
*was put forth as an example,*
*your people turned away from it...*
*He was no more than a servant*
*whom we blessed,*
*and We made him an example...*
*And he was a lesson for the Hour.*
*So have no doubt about it.*
*And follow Me; this is a straight path...*
*And when Jesus came with proofs, he said:*
*"I have come to you with the wisdom,*
*and to clarify some of the matters*
*in which you dispute.*
*So be aware of God and obey me."*

Qur'an 43:57-63

So Jesus was an example or a lesson of how to be a blessed servant and follow God's straight path. He also was to clarify with wisdom things that we dispute about. What is it we dispute so often in religious circles? The character of God. So Jesus' example was to show us the character of God which is why he will be a lesson for us all the way to the Hour of Judgment. He will also be a witness for or against us depending on whether we have followed his example, become aware of God and obeyed Jesus.

*And from the people of the Book*
*are those who refused to believe in him [Jesus]*
*before his death*
*and on the Day of Resurrection*
*he will be a witness against them.*

Qur'an 4:159

Jesus was a sign for believers from the day of his birth. Who could deny the power of God to create a miracle in the womb of a virgin? Then who could deny God's power in the miracles that Jesus performed: healing the sick, chasing out demons and raising the dead? Who could deny the example that Jesus gave of God's love for sinners and His mercy in the forgiving of their sins? Jesus' life was filled with signs for those believers with eyes to see and ears to hear. God made Jesus such a significant sign for the worlds because He wanted people to see a living parable of His character.

The greatest sign of God's character was the greatest love that he has for his creatures as demonstrated by Jesus laying down his life for his friends. Then the greatest sign of God's power was demonstrating that not only does He have the power to take life (as he did by his plan to terminate Jesus' life [*mutawaffeeka*]), but He demonstrated that He has the power to give life to the dead when He raised Jesus back to life and took him to heaven to await the Day of Judgment.

*...And We shall make him [Jesus]*
*a sign for the people*
*and a mercy from Us.*
*It is a matter already ordained.*

Qur'an 19:21

## **CONCLUSION**

In conclusion, the Jesus of the Qur'an and the Gospels is a sign for all peoples in that he is a miraculous example of the character of God. He lived a parable of who God was and is by performing miraculous signs of healing, casting out demons and raising the dead to life. Ultimately, the biggest reason Jesus is a sign for believers is that he showed God's character of love by laying down his life for his friends and by showing the example of God's power over death through his resurrection. Because God used him as a sign, Jesus was raised to heaven to be a witness for God on the Day of Judgment and Resurrection.

# Messenger

*And eternal life is this:*
*to know you, the one true God,*
*and him whom you sent,*
*Yeshua [Jesus] the Messiah.*

John 17:3 (CJB)

*...Jesus, Son of Mary,*
*was no more than a messenger of God*
*and the fulfillment of His word to Mary*
*and a Spirit from Him...*

Qur'an 4:171

*The Messiah, Son of Mary,*
*is no more than a messenger;*
*like whom messengers have passed away;...*

Qur'an 5:75

In Islam a messenger (*rasul*) was a prophet sent with a specific message for a specific people at a specific time. Five of the messengers were given scriptures as well: Abraham, Moses, David, Jesus and Muhammad (PBUH). So when the Qur'an says that Jesus was no more than a messenger, it means he was one of the elite few selected by God with messages for humanity important enough to have been written down in the Holy Scriptures.

The important thing for us as believers is to know and understand the messages of the messengers since that is why they were sent. The Qur'an is primarily the message God sent through the angel Gabriel to Muhammad (PBUH), and then to the Arabs and the rest of the world. Therefore, the Qur'an only alludes to the specifics of the message given to Jesus in one place.

*And We sent Jesus, Son of Mary*
*and We gave him the Gospel,*
*and We ordained in the hearts of his followers*
*kindness and mercy...*
*O you who believe, you shall reverence God*
*and believe in His messenger.*
*He will then grant you double*
*the reward from His mercy,*
*and He will make for you a light*
*by which you shall walk,*
*and He will forgive you.*
*And God is Forgiving, Merciful.*
*So that the followers of the Book should know*
*that they have no power over the grace of God,*
*and that all grace is in the hand of God.*
*He bestows it upon whoever He wills.*
*God is Possessor of Infinite Grace.*

Qur'an 57:27-29

Jesus' essential message had to do with kindness and mercy, the kindness and mercy of God. Unfortunately, over the years, people claiming to be followers of Jesus and calling themselves Christians had come to think that they had power over this grace of God. Priests and Christian leaders made the people believe they only had access to the grace and mercy of God through human intercessors and only through their religion.

So the message sent to Muhammad (PBUH) was to clear this up and remind the hearers of the Qur'an that God's forgiveness, mercy and grace are available to all believers no matter what religion they belong to. This is the essence of God's character: love, mercy, grace, and forgiveness.

The first thing Jesus did was to clarify some of the misunderstandings people had about God in the Old Testament (*Tawrat* and *Zaboor*).

*And when Jesus, Son of Mary, said:*
*"O children of Israel, I am a messenger of God to you,*
*authenticating what is between*
*my hands of the Torah...*

Qur'an 61:6

This message was fleshed out in the Gospels (*Injeel*). Of course, the Gospels are long and the complete message can only be understood by reading all the Gospels. However, a few examples will help to understand the essence.

The first of Jesus' epic sermons where he proclaims the message given to him by God is found in Matthew 5-7. The following is a sampling of that message:

*Blessed are the poor in spirit:*
*for theirs is the kingdom of heaven.*
*Blessed are they that mourn:*
*for they shall be comforted.*
*Blessed are the meek:*
*for they shall inherit the earth.*
*Blessed are they which do hunger*
*and thirst after righteousness:*
*for they shall be filled.*
*Blessed are the merciful:*
*for they shall obtain mercy.*
*Blessed are the pure in heart:*
*for they shall see God.*
*Blessed are the peacemakers:*
*for they shall be called the children of God.*
*Blessed are they which are persecuted*
*for righteousness' sake:*
*for theirs is the kingdom of heaven.*
*Blessed are ye, when men shall revile you,*
*and persecute you, and shall say all manner of evil*
*against you falsely, for my sake.*
*Rejoice, and be exceeding glad:*
*for great is your reward in heaven:*
*for so persecuted they the prophets which were before you...*

*Think not that I am come*
*to destroy the law, or the prophets:*
*I am not come to destroy, but to fulfill.*
*For verily I say unto you,*
*Till heaven and earth pass,*
*one jot or one tittle shall in no wise pass from the law,*
*till all be fulfilled...*

*Ye have heard that it was said of them of old time,*
*Thou shalt not kill; and whosoever shall kill*
*shall be in danger of the judgment:*
*But I say unto you,*
*That whosoever is angry with his brother*
*without a cause shall be in danger of the judgment...*

*Ye have heard that it was said by them of old time,*
*Thou shalt not commit adultery:*
*But I say unto you,*
*That whosoever looketh on a woman to lust after her*
*hath committed adultery with her already in his heart...*

*Ye have heard that it hath been said,*
*An eye for an eye, and a tooth for a tooth:*
*But I say unto you,*
*That ye resist not evil:*
*but whosoever shall smite thee on thy right cheek,*
*turn to him the other also...*

*Ye have heard that it hath been said,*
*Thou shalt love thy neighbour, and hate thine enemy.*
*But I say unto you,*
*Love your enemies,*
*bless them that curse you,*
*do good to them that hate you,*
*and pray for them*
*which despitefully use you, and persecute you;...*

Matthew 5 (KJV)

Jesus turns human ideas of morality on their head. The blessed are not the rich, happy, strong, satisfied, popular and war-like, but rather the poor, the mourning, the meek, the hungry, the merciful, the peacemakers, the pure, and the persecuted.

Jesus then goes on to say that all the commandments of God are more than rules; they're matters of the heart and mind. It's not enough to not kill, we shouldn't be angry. It's not enough to not commit an act of adultery, we shouldn't even think about it in the privacy of our rooms or in our minds. It's not enough to be fair and just, we should accept when people treat us wrong and not retaliate. And it's not enough to love our friends and family, we need to love our enemies, bless them, do good to them and pray for them.

Jesus sets the standard of righteousness high, but he doesn't end his message without hope. John 14-17 is Jesus' last sermon to his disciples before the end of his earthly mission. Jesus calls God his Father, not in the biological sense, but rather in the sense of a God who provides, educates, takes care of His created beings (i.e. His children).

*Let not your heart be troubled:*
*ye believe in God, believe also in me.*
*In my Father's house are many mansions:*
*if it were not so, I would have told you.*
*I go to prepare a place for you.*
*And if I go and prepare a place for you,*
*I will come again, and receive you unto myself;*
*that where I am, there ye may be also.*
*And whither I go ye know, and the way ye know...*

*...he that hath seen me hath seen the Father;*
*and how sayest thou then, Show us the Father?*
*Believest thou not that I am in the Father,*
*and the Father in me?*
*the words that I speak unto you I speak not of myself:*
*but the Father that dwelleth in me, he doeth the works.*
*Believe me that I am in the Father, and the Father in me:*
*or else believe me for the very works' sake.*
*Verily, verily, I say unto you,*
*He that believeth on me,*
*the works that I do shall he do also;*
*and greater works than these shall he do;*
*because I go unto my Father.*
*And whatsoever ye shall ask in my name, that will I do,*
*that the Father may be glorified in the son.*
*If ye shall ask any thing in my name, I will do it.*

John 14:1-14 (KJV)

This message is very deep and yet simple at the same time. Jesus gives us hope, because in God's house (Paradise) there are many mansions and if we believe in God we have a place there through God's mercy and grace. The message of Jesus bringing to light the character of God as a God of love and forgiveness is the truth and the way to find eternal life.

Jesus, by being filled with the Spirit of God (God's essence and character) was able to represent to human beings what God is like. So by seeing how Jesus treats sick people and outcasts and the poor and the oppressed and how he heals them and has mercy on them and forgives them we can understand that this is God's character as well.

We can trust that Jesus was sent by God as a messenger because of the miracles Jesus did through God's power working through him. And if we put our entire trust and faith in God, we can do even greater works through that same power that comes from God.

*"But the Advocate, the Holy Spirit,*
*whom the Father will send in my name,*
*will teach you all things and will remind you*
*of everything I have said to you.*
*Peace I leave with you; my peace I give you.*
*I do not give to you as the world gives.*
*Do not let your hearts be troubled and do not be afraid.*

*You heard me say,*
*'I am going away and I am coming back to you.'*
*If you loved me, you would be glad*
*that I am going to the Father,*
*for the Father is greater than I.*
*I have told you now before it happens,*
*so that when it does happen you will believe.*

*I will not say much more to you,*
*for the prince of this world is coming.*
*He has no hold over me,*
*but he comes so that the world may learn*
*that I love the Father and do exactly*
*what my Father has commanded me..."*

John 14:26-31 (NIV)

There is more truth to learn and more messages to come through the Spirit of God who will teach us and remind us of previous messages. Jesus' message was also one of peace and the removal of fear from our hearts because Jesus was going to be raised up to God before coming back to judge the world.

God is greater than Jesus. The life of Jesus clearly reveals the fact that He depended every day of his life on a Power that was beyond him. He had to tap into that Power each and every day. He existed because of God. He did the miracles because of God and after his death, it was God who raised him up and took him to Paradise. Jesus had power because he loved God and did exactly what God commanded him to do. Jesus reveals the true character of God: love and understanding.

*My command is this:*
*Love each other as I have loved you.*
*Greater love has no one than this:*
*to lay down one's life for one's friends.*
*You are my friends if you do what I command.*
*I no longer call you servants,*
*because a servant does not know his master's business.*
*Instead, I have called you friends,*
*for everything that I learned from my Father*
*I have made known to you.*

John 15:12-15 (NIV)

While we are to respect God and submit to Him, ultimately he desires our friendship and freely given love. Love cannot be forced, so God prefers friends who understand His purposes and plans. To love someone you have to be their friend. To be their friend you have to trust them. To trust them you have to know them. To know someone you have to spend time with them and converse with them.

So, by putting His Spirit in Jesus, he allowed us to see His character in three dimensions so we could know Him, then trust Him, then befriend Him, then love Him. And to aid that process God showed that His love for us is the greatest love there is, to give up one's life for a friend. Yet God can't die, so He created Jesus and put His Spirit in him so that we could see that God is willing to die for us if He could die, that's how much God loves us.

## CONCLUSION

In conclusion, the Jesus of the Qur'an and the Gospels is a messenger of God sent with the specific message of clarifying the previous scriptures and teaching believers about the mercy, forgiveness, grace and love of God by living out God's character in three dimensions through the empowerment of the indwelling Spirit of God going so far as to die to show that God's love is the greatest love of all. And this message was important enough to have been written down in what we call the Gospels (*Injeel*).

# The Second Adam

*The example of Jesus with God
is similar to that of Adam;
He created him from dust,
then said to him "Be" and he was.*

Qur'an 3:59

*For since death came through a man,
also the resurrection of the dead has come through a man.
For just as in connection with Adam all die,
so in connection with the Messiah all will be made alive.*

I Corinthians 15:21-22 (CJB)

Let's go back to the interesting comparison made in both the Qur'an and the Gospels between Jesus and Adam. In the Qur'an, both are said to be different than other human beings in not being created through the normal human process of procreation with a human father and mother but rather through a direct creative word from God: "Be," and they were (*kun faya kun*).

*The example of Jesus with God
is similar to that of Adam;
He created him from dust,
then said to him "Be" and he was.*

Qur'an 3:59

*She said, "My Lord!
How can I have a son,
when no man has touched me?"*

*"Thus does God create at will:*
*when God decides on something,*
*God simply says to it 'Be!'*
*and it is.*

Qur'an 3:47

In the Gospels, both are called the "Son of God" relating to the fact that they had no father in the human sense but were directly created by God.

*Which was the son of Enos,*
*which was the son of Seth,*
*which was the son of Adam,*
*which was the Son of God.*

Luke 3:38 (KJV)

*And Mary said to the angel,*
*"How will this be, since I am a virgin?"*
*And the angel answered her,*
*"The Holy Spirit will come upon you,*
*and the power of the Most High*
*will overshadow you;*
*therefore the child to be born*
*will be called holy—the Son of God.*

Luke 1:34-35 (ESV)

So at the beginning of the world, God creates a man, Adam, directly without passing through the process of human procreation to demonstrate His creative genius and His plan for humanity. Then, when humans had gone way off of the straight path, God creates another man, Jesus, with His powerful Word. This "Second Adam's" mission is to bring humanity back to the worship of the true God by displaying God's character through his life.

The Gospels explain this relation between the "First Adam" and the "Second Adam" (Jesus):

*Sin came into the world because of what one man did.*
*And with sin came death.*
*So this is why all people must die—*

*because all people have sinned.*
*Sin was in the world before the Law of Moses.*
*But God does not consider people*
*guilty of sin if there is no law.*
*But from the time of Adam to the time of Moses,*
*everyone had to die.*
*Adam died because he sinned*
*by not obeying God's command.*
*But even those who did not sin that same way had to die.*

*That one man, Adam,*
*can be compared to Christ,*
*the one who was coming in the future.*
*But God's free gift is not like Adam's sin.*
*Many people died because of the sin of that one man.*
*But the grace that people received*
*from God was much greater.*
*Many received God's gift of life*
*by the grace of this other man, Jesus Christ.*

*After Adam sinned once,*
*he was judged guilty.*
*But the gift of God is different.*
*His free gift came after many sins,*
*and it makes people right with him.*
*One man sinned, and so death ruled*
*all people because of that one man.*
*But now some people accept God's full grace*
*and his great gift of being made right.*
*Surely they will have true life*
*and rule through the one man, Jesus Christ.*

*So that one sin of Adam brought*
*the punishment of death to all people.*
*But in the same way, Christ did something so good*
*that it makes all people right with God.*
*And that brings them true life.*
*One man disobeyed God and many became sinners.*
*But in the same way, one man obeyed God*
*and many will be made right.*
*The law was brought in so that*
*more people would sin the way Adam did.*

*But where sin increased,*
*there was even more of God's grace.*
*Sin once used death to rule us.*
*But God gave us more of his grace*
*so that grace could rule*
*by making us right with him.*
*And this brings us eternal life*
*through Jesus Christ our Lord.*

Romans 5:12-21 (ERV)

Adam disobeyed God's command and lost his place in Paradise with access to the Tree of Life. As a consequence of his disobedience, Adam eventually died. All his descendants, born in the natural way of cohabitation with a woman, also ended up dying because they had no more access to the Tree of Life either (See Qur'an 7:11-25 and the Torah, Genesis 3:1-24).

So God, who loves his created beings, intervened again with another miraculous man: Jesus, born of a virgin, bypassing the normal route of human reproduction. By living a life of obedience to God, Jesus undid the disobedient act of Adam and brought the gift of God's grace back into reach of humanity.

*Who in the days of his flesh,*
*when he [Jesus] had offered up prayers*
*and supplications with strong crying and tears*
*unto him that was able to save him from death,*
*and was heard in that he feared;*
*Though he were a son, yet learned he obedience*
*by the things which he suffered;*
*And being made perfect,*
*he became the author of eternal salvation*
*unto all them that obey him.*

Hebrews 5:7-9 (KJV)

When the angel Gabriel announced Jesus' birth to the virgin Mary, he stated that Jesus would be a gift, first to Mary as a pure son, but then to all people as a sign and mercy from God.

*He said: "I am the messenger of your Lord,*
*to grant you the gift of a pure son."*

*She [Mary] said: "How can I have a son*
*when no human being has been with me,*
*nor have I desired such?"*
*He said: "It is such that your Lord has said,*
*it is easy for Me.*
*And We shall make him a sign for the people*
*and a mercy from Us.*
*It is a matter already ordained."*

Qur'an 19:19-21

The gift of purity that man had been searching for since Adam strayed from the straight path, God gave through the miracle of Jesus bringing mercy and grace back within reach of all humanity. He wants to give us the same gift that he gave Mary: purity that can only come as a gift from God.

*So it is written:*
*"The first man Adam became a living being";*
*the last Adam, a life-giving spirit.*
*The spiritual did not come first,*
*but the natural, and after that the spiritual.*
*The first man was of the dust of the earth;*
*the second man is of heaven.*
*As was the earthly man,*
*so are those who are of the earth;*
*and as is the heavenly man,*
*so also are those who are of heaven.*
*And just as we have borne the image of the earthly man,*
*so shall we bear the image of the heavenly man.*

I Corinthians 15:45-49 (NIV)

There is a difference between Adam and Jesus, however. Adam was formed from the dust of the ground and then had the breath of life breathed into him. Jesus was created as an embryo in a virgin's womb and then had God's Spirit placed in him. This having the Holy Spirit in him allowed Jesus to give life to the dead through the power of God; he became a "life-giving spirit."

*...and I [Jesus]...give life to the dead*
*with the permission of God,...*

Qur'an 3:49

When Adam died, he went back to the dust where he awaits the Day of Resurrection. Jesus, however, was raised after only a few days in the tomb and was taken to heaven to be with God until he returns on the Day of Resurrection. So Adam is earthly and Jesus is heavenly. We are all borne with earthly bodies, but on the Day of Resurrection, if we have accepted the gift of purity from God and stayed on the straight path, we will be given a heavenly body.

*And We sent Jesus, Son of Mary*
*and We gave him the Gospel,*
*and We ordained in the hearts of his followers*
*kindness and mercy...*
*all grace is in the hand of God.*
*He bestows it upon whoever He wills.*
*God is Possessor of Infinite Grace.*

Qur'an 57:27-29

## <u>CONCLUSION</u>

In conclusion, the Jesus of the Qur'an and the Gospels is compared to Adam in that both came into existence by the miracle of a direct, creative word of God (*kun faya kun*). However, Jesus is different in that while Adam disobeyed God and was chased from Paradise, Jesus obeyed God and became the vehicle God uses for bestowing the gift of His grace and mercy on us so we can obtain the purity we can never get through our own efforts.

Both the Qur'an and the Gospels plainly tell us that the first Adam, the one that was created out of the dust, disobeyed and lost Paradise while the Second Adam, Jesus, obeyed and gained Paradise. The choice is ours. We can follow the First Adam and find death or follow the Second Adam and find life in Paradise.

# Epilogue

*From one man he made all the nations,*
*that they should inhabit the whole earth;*
*and he marked out their appointed times in history*
*and the boundaries of their lands.*
*God did this so that they would seek him*
*and perhaps reach out for him and find him,*
*though he is not far from any one of us.*

Acts 17:26-27 (NIV)

*...if God had willed*
*He would have made you all one nation,*
*but He tests you with what*
*He has given you;*
*so strive to do good.*
*To God you will return all of you,*
*and He will inform you regarding*
*that in which you dispute.*

Qur'an 5:48

In conclusion, the Jesus of the Qur'an and the Gospels is the same. So what does this mean? Does it mean we all have to become the same? Do we start a new religion? How should this impact us as true believers?

I believe it should start by making us stop fighting each other. Throughout the centuries there have been so many misunderstandings. So many innocent lives have been lost and killed all in the name of Islam and Christianity. Wars have been fought and infidels from both camps have been exterminated systematically, without prejudice and mercy.

So many wars have been fought and justified because we can each see the other as the enemy because of misconceptions about Jesus. Muslims can justify killing the Christian "infidels" because they believe in three gods instead of One. Christians excuse the massacre of Muslim "infidels" because they don't believe the "truth" about Jesus' special role.

But if Jesus is actually the same in both the Qur'an and the Gospels, then we can no longer justify suicide bombings, slander, burning of the Qur'an or the Bible, prejudice, hate, or propaganda.

However, that doesn't mean we all have to be the same. God loves variety. No two snowflakes are the same, nothing in nature is. How much less the crowning act of Creation: humankind. As Acts 17:26-27 and Qur'an 5:48 tell us, God's plan was for us to be different nations, peoples, cultures, languages, and religions. It was He who placed us where we were born and at what time in history. Why? So we could seek and find God who is not far from any one of us.

> *And We have created man*
> *and We know what his soul whispers to him,*
> *and We are closer to him than his jugular vein.*

> Qur'an 50:16

The good news is we can stop trying to convert each other. We can each stay in our own cultural background where God has so divinely and specially placed us. We ought to dialogue together because we each have much to learn. The Christian believer should strive to help his Muslim brother be a better Muslim and vice versa.

What do we have to gain if in the long run our intolerance towards each other's beliefs shows no room for mercy or kindness? On the judgment day how can we stand in the Presence of a blameless God who judges all hearts, if we approach Him with impure acts and bold arrogance? How can a limitless God who created the Infinite Universe be limited to our specific understanding of Him and how can there be no room for God to exist other than in the myopic hallways of our blindness?

God is beyond our understanding. All we can understand from the Qur'an and the Gospels is that Jesus the Messiah was born through a miraculous event. He lived a life in total submission to God. He was kind and loving. He healed the sick and raised the dead. His thoughts were first for the welfare of others. After his death, God in His mercy took him to heaven. Thus, we too can have that same chance of an entry to Paradise, if we follow the example of the Messiah as penned in the Qur'an and the Gospels.

Let me conclude with an illustration. There once were three blind men who were taken to see an elephant. None of them had ever heard of such a creature and so they were eager to learn about the animal in the only way they knew how: by touch and feel.

The first blind man approached the head and ran his hand along the trunk of the beast.

"Ah ha!" he exclaimed. "The elephant is like a large python!"

But the second blind man who had been feeling the legs of the elephant quickly contradicted him.

"No, no, my friend," he said. "You are mistaken. The elephant is like a tree trunk, strong and firm."

Laughing condescendingly, the third blind man reproached his colleagues. "Nay, nay, good chaps," he chuckled pleasantly as he released the elephants tail that he had been stroking. "The elephant is like a tree BRANCH, gently swaying in the wind."

Each man was blind. His perception was limited. Each was convinced the others were wrong and only he was right. The truth, for those whose eyes were opened, was that all were right because the elephant was much bigger than each of their limited points of view.

We need each other if we are to enlarge our view of the Great God who is our Master. Only by seeing God through the eyes of our brothers and sisters can we get to know Him better. Rather than arguing and disputing we should be sharing and learning. God's revelation of Himself is progressive. He has revealed the truth through countless messengers, prophets and Holy Books.

> *We have sent down the Torah,*
> *in it is a guidance and a light;*
> *the prophets who have submitted judged with it*
> *for those who are Jewish,*
> *and the Devotees, and the Priests,*
> *for what they were entrusted of the Book of God,*
> *and they were witness over.*
> *So do not be concerned with the people*
> *but be concerned with Me;*
> *and do not purchase with My revelations a cheap price.*
> *And whoever does not judge with what*
> *God has sent down,*
> *then these are the rejecters...*

> *And We sent in their footsteps Jesus, Son of Mary,*
> *authenticating what was present with him of the Torah.*

*And We gave him the Gospel*
*in it is a guidance and a light,*
*and authenticating what was present*
*with him of the Torah*
*and a guidance and a lesson for the righteous*
*And let the people of the Gospel*
*judge with what God has sent down in it.*
*And whoever does not judge with what*
*God has sent down,*
*then these are the wicked.*

*And We have sent down to you the Book*
*with the truth,*
*authenticating what is between your hands*
*of the Book and superseding it.*
*So judge between them by*
*what God has sent down,*
*and do not follow their desires*
*from what has come to you of the truth.*
*For each of you We have made laws, and a structure;*
*and if God had willed*
*He would have made you all one nation,*
*but He tests you with what*
*He has given you;*
*so strive to do good.*
*To God you will return all of you,*
*and He will inform you regarding*
*that in which you dispute.*

Qur'an 5:44-48

Ultimately, all these revelations are so we can know God, and knowing Him trust Him, and trusting Him submit to Him, and submitting to Him come out of darkness into the light.

*God is the ally of those who believe,*
*He brings them out of the darkness*
*and into the light...*

Qur'an 2:257

*But if our gospel be hid,*

*it is hid to them that are lost:*
*In whom the god of this world hath blinded*
*the minds of them which believe not,*
*lest the light of the glorious gospel of Christ,*
*who is the image of God,*
*should shine unto them...*

*For God, who commanded the light*
*to shine out of darkness,*
*hath shined in our hearts,*
*to give the light of the knowledge*
*of the glory of God*
*in the face of Jesus Christ.*

2 Corinthians 4:3-6 (KJV)

## WHAT NOW?

Where do we go from here? I suggest that first of all, we begin with conversation, debate and dialogue. If this book has stimulated your thinking, share it with others of all faiths and get some reconciliation going. Start a group of like minded believers to learn from each other and grow in faith as you attempt to follow the example of the Messiah. Or join our online forum (http://jesusqurangospels.freeforums.net), post your comments and let's learn from each other. As the Scriptures say:

*Come now, and let us reason together...*

Isaiah 1:18 (KJV)

*As iron sharpens iron, so one person sharpens another.*

Proverbs 27:17 (NIV)

*...It is thus that God clarifies for you the revelations that you may think.*

Qur'an 2:219

# Selected Readings

The following are books that have inspired or contributed to the author's reflections on the Jesus of the Qur'an and the Gospels.

1. A Deadly Misunderstanding: A Congressman's Quest to Bridge the Muslim-Christian Divide by Mark D. Siljander & John David Mann (Oct 7, 2008)
2. Jesus in the Qur'an by Geoffrey Parrinder (May 1, 1995)
3. Muhammad by Karen Armstrong (Sep 10, 1993)
4. The Desire of Ages by Ellen G. White (2006)
5. The Road to Mecca by Muhammad Asad (Jan 1, 2000)
6. Allah, Liberty and Love: The Courage to Reconcile Faith and Freedom by Irshad Manji (Jun 14, 2011)
7. Pilgrims of Christ on the Muslim Road: Exploring a New Path Between Two Faiths by Paul-Gordon Chandler Nov 16, 2008)
8. Allah: A Christian Response by Miroslav Volf (Feb 7, 2012)
9. Children of the East: The Spiritual Heritage of Islam in the Bible by James Appel, MD (Jul 6, 2011)
10. The Qur'an: A New Translation by Thomas Cleary (Apr 1, 2004)
11. Le Christ de l'Islam. by Michel Hayek.(1959)
12. The Girl with the Dove Tattoo by Brian D. McLaren (Jun 25, 2012)
13. Why Did Jesus, Moses, the Buddha, and Mohammed Cross the Road? by Brian D. McLaren (Sep 11, 2012)
14. Arabs in the Shadow of Israel: The Unfolding of God's Prophetic Plan for Ishmael's Line by Tony Maalouf (Nov 10, 2003)

# About the Author

James Appel, MD holds a Bachelor of Arts in Theology from Southern Adventist University and a Doctor of Medicine from the Loma Linda University School of Medicine. He completed a three year residency in Family Practice at the Ventura County Medical Center in California. He has spent the last nine years working as a physician and surgeon in the Republic of Chad. It was in Chad that he was introduced to Islam and began studying the Qur'an and other books on Muslims. Coming from a long line of Christian Ministers and Missionaries, Dr. Appel grew up in an environment where thinking about and debating spirituality and religion was part of the family heritage. James is married to a Danish nurse, Sarah, and together they have a daughter, Miriam, and a newborn son, Noah.

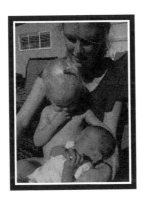

Made in the USA
San Bernardino, CA
22 July 2015